Enjoy

A Thirst-Quenching Look at Philippians

Tianne Moon

LifeWay Press®
Nashville, Tennessee

Published by LifeWay Press®. © 2004 Fellowship Church

No part of this book may be reproduced or transmitted in any form or by any means, electronic or mechanical, including photocopying and recording, or by any information storage or retrieval system, except as may be expressly permitted in writing by the publisher. Requests for permission should be addressed in writing to LifeWay Press®; One LifeWay Plaza; Nashville, TN 37234-0175.

ISBN 0-6331-9841-2

This book is course CG–1050 in the Biblical Studies category
of the Christian Growth Study Plan.

Dewey Decimal Classification Number: 227.6

Subject Headings:
BIBLE. N.T. PHILIPPIANS--STUDY \ JOY AND SORROW \ WOMEN—RELIGIOUS LIFE

Unless otherwise noted, all Scripture quotations are taken from the *Holman Christian Standard Bible*®, © Copyright 2001 Holman Bible Publishers, Nashville, TN. Used by permission.

Scripture quotations identified NIV are taken from *The New International Version* © International Bible Publishers 1973, 1978, 1984. Used by permission.

To order additional copies of this resource, WRITE to LifeWay Church Resources
Customer Service; One LifeWay Plaza; Nashville, TN 37234-0013;
FAX (615) 251-5933; PHONE (800) 458-2772;
E-MAIL *customerservice@lifeway.com*; ORDER ONLINE at *www.lifeway.com*;
or VISIT the LifeWay Christian Store serving you.

Printed in the United States of America

Leadership and Adult Publishing
LifeWay Church Resources
One LifeWay Plaza
Nashville, TN 37234-0175

Contents

About the Authors

Born and raised in Texas as a "preacher's kid," Tianne attended Baylor University and graduated from The University of Texas School of Allied Health Sciences with a degree in Physical Therapy. She practiced as a physical therapist for eight years before joining the staff of Fellowship Church, Grapevine, Texas, in 1999 as Spiritual Development Coordinator. She continues to serve in that role today.

Her current responsibilities include coordinating women's ministries and developing adult Bible study teachers and curriculum. A member of Fellowship since 1991, Tianne has also been active in the church's music, singles, and small-group ministries.

Tianne is a graduate of Dallas Theological Seminary with a Master of Arts in Biblical Studies. She currently lives in Flower Mound, Texas, with her husband, Mike, and their two dogs, Bishop and Bypass.

Michelle King, author of the leader guide for *Enjoy* uses her education-based background to lead Bible studies in Edwards Road Baptist Church in Greenville, South Carolina. She believes that no Bible study should be just a time-filler or another book to take up space on the shelf.

Michelle delights in using fun activities to help students remember and apply what they learn to their own lives. Believing that Jesus Christ used the word *disciple* to mean student or learner in addition to follower, Michelle strives to help us be first and foremost—His learners.

DO WHAT YOU HAVE LEARNED AND RECEIVED AND HEARD AND SEEN IN ME, AND THE GOD OF PEACE WILL BE WITH YOU.

PHILIPPIANS 4:9

Introduction

Texas has some intensely hot summer days. When I am in the middle of one of those days, perspiring and longing for a cool breeze, nothing refreshes me like an ice cold glass of lemonade! But I've noticed that even though that drink is refreshing, it doesn't actually change my circumstances. I still perspire and it is still intensely hot, but it's just that I feel a little better in the midst of it all. Lemonade can go a long way in getting me through the heat!

We sometimes find ourselves in the middle of pretty intense circumstances that leave us longing for a fresh, cool breeze. Often we desire something to get us through the heat and God's joy does exactly that—it refreshes us. While the joy that comes from the Lord does not necessarily change your current circumstances, it can help you feel better in the midst of them.

As we are about to discover together, joy does not come from a change in our circumstances. It comes from a change in our perspective on those circumstances.

But where does joy come from? And how can we get more of it? Let's satisfy our thirst with an in-depth look ...

Jeanne

About the Study

Enjoy: A Thirst-Quenching Look at Philippians has two major purposes:
(1) To help participants discover how to experience joy in every season of their lives; and
(2) To equip participants to study the Bible for themselves, experiencing its power and developing a passion for knowing God.

Enjoy is based on a discovery process known as *inductive Bible study* which encourages participants to study selected Scriptures (in our case, primarily from Philippians) to draw logical conclusions about how those verses apply to life. The greatest benefit is gained by asking God to teach you and making a commitment to do the work that is required. If you find this Bible study to be different, then celebrate those differences and anticipate the new directions and insights God will show you.

Tianne reflects on the need to keep Bible study fresh and meaningful. "After many years of studying and teaching the Bible, I found myself getting into a rut: read the passage, make some notes, organize my thoughts, practice teaching the lesson. My process had become so predictable that I no longer experienced the thrill and excitement I had felt in earlier years. I approached the text with my head, but not with my heart.

"So I took fresh, creative approaches to Bible study. Suddenly Scripture came alive before my eyes; passages I had studied took on new life."

The approaches that make Bible study come alive for Tianne comprise her "toolbox"—eight Bible study tools you will be introduced to and taught to use. As Tianne introduces a tool, she gives an opportunity, involving one or more portions of Philippians, to use it. When she adds a new tool, she gives opportunities to use the new tool plus the other tools. Later you'll have the opportunity to choose the tools you think are most appropriate for a particular passage.

You'll get feedback on how you're doing as you talk to the other participants in your small group, view the video, and (as needed) compare your answers to Tianne's. As you involve yourself in the study's unique approach, you will find yourself becoming proficient in using the tools. A greater benefit to adopting Tianne's tools is the confidence you'll develop in your ability to study other parts of the Bible for yourself. In the back of your book is a Toolbox bookmark you can place in your Bible as you apply your new tools. Selected verses from our study can help you with Scripture memorization.

"My passion for Bible study was ignited when others equipped me to unwrap this beautiful gift for myself."

—Tianne Moon

This study is designed so that anyone can participate—even those who have never set foot in a church. *Enjoy* provides a great opportunity to involve women who have no previous church relationships without excluding those who have grown up in church. It can help participants develop an initial thirst for the Bible and for God. The relationships that grow out of such a Bible study can help women become interested in church fellowship.

Enjoy is a six-week study. Each session includes both small-group discussion and large-group video teaching and lasts approximately one hour. The video teaching sets the stage for the following week's home assignments. Each weekly session is comprised of these elements:

- *Welcome* (5 min.)—The Leader Kit includes DVD video. Depending on the size of your group and your leader's preferences, you may use Tianne's video overviews. (Some leaders may prefer to show this segment to their small-group leaders before the session.) This clip serves as an introduction to your weekly group time and leads into small-group discussion.
- *Small-Group Discussion* (20 min.)—Your small-group time offers inter-active learning activities and provides an opportunity to look back and discuss how you are applying the previous week's home assignments. This is also a great time to share prayer requests.
- *Large-Group Video Teaching* (25 min.)—The video teaching time intro-duces new material for the upcoming week's home assignments. A viewer guide allows you to follow along and take notes.
- *Closing*—Prayer and announcements end most sessions.

This workbook, moving verse-by-verse through the Book of Philippians, offers five days of study material for you to read and apply to your life. It includes five weeks of daily home assignments, with week 6 being a video session only. Through these assignments, you will be introduced to eight tools that will help you in personal Bible study. Each day's assignment should take about 20 minutes. Continue to meet with your group even if you have not been able to complete all the home assignments.

Exceptional Joy in an Ordinary Life

VIEWER GUIDE

OUR PURPOSE IMPACTS OUR PERSPECTIVE ON THE CIRCUMSTANCES OF OUR LIVES

Our purpose drives our _____.

Four Ways Paul's Life Changed:

1. Paul's purpose impacted the way he saw

   his _____ (Phil. 1:13-14).

2. Paul's purpose changed his view on

   _____ (1:15-18).

3. Paul's purpose impacted the way he viewed _____

   and _____ (1:21-26).

4. Paul's purpose impacted the way he viewed

   his _____ (1:27-28).

God's purpose for your life is to _____ _____.

> *"Live your life in a manner worthy*
> *of the gospel of Christ."*
> *Philippians 1:27*

A Thirst-Quenching Look at Your Life's Purpose

As I shopped for sunglasses recently, I was amazed by the wide variety of available lenses. They come in almost any color! It was fun to see how people and the setting around me seemed to change as I peered through different lenses. But I knew that though the colors changed, my surroundings really didn't. Though looking through colored lenses made me see things in a different way, the things I was seeing were still the same.

Do you need to get a new perspective on your life? Do your current circumstances bore you to tears, stretch you to your limit, or stress you to the max? If so, it is time to see your life through new lenses.

The Book of Philippians is a letter written by the Apostle Paul. In this letter to his friends in Philippi, he teaches and encourages them to get a new perspective on life. Paul knew that the only way to experience thirst-quenching joy that fully satisfies is by getting God's perspective on life.

This week we will walk through the first chapter of Philippians. Here Paul begins by explaining his circumstances and continues by sharing with his readers a new perspective on those challenging circumstances. As you catch a glimpse of Paul's purpose, I hope you will realize that a God-centered focus on your life's purpose will give you a new perspective and will help you experience joy too—regardless of life's circumstances.

Spending time studying the Bible is an important key to getting God's perspective. The Bible is God's guidebook, and it helps us see our lives and our world through His eyes. I have included some Bible study tools each week, and I hope they will help you learn how to understand and study this awesome Book.

Hold on tight! You are in for quite a ride as you learn how the God who created you with a divine and unique purpose can satisfy your deepest thirst.

Day 1 Aligning My Life with Truth

Have you ever thought while listening to someone teach the Bible, *Wow! When I read the Bible, I don't see all of that! If only I could understand Scripture like she does!* If so, be encouraged. One of the purposes of this study is to help you become more comfortable with studying the Bible on your own. I want to help you see all that God wants to communicate to you so you can discover truths of His Word for yourself rather than having to wait for someone else to show them to you.

Many of us don't study the Bible on our own because we doubt that we can understand it and we are fearful that we might misinterpret it. Let's take a moment to see what the Bible itself says about that.

Read John 14:23-27.

> ²³Jesus answered, "If anyone loves Me, he will keep My word. My Father will love him, and We will come to him and make Our home with him. ²⁴The one who doesn't love Me will not keep My words. The word that you hear is not Mine but is from the Father who sent Me. ²⁵"I have spoken these things to you while I remain with you. ²⁶But the Counselor, the Holy Spirit—the Father will send in My name—will teach you all things and remind you of everything I have told you. ²⁷"Peace I leave with you. My peace I give to you. I do not give to you as the world gives. Your heart must not be troubled or fearful."

Circle what verses 25–26 promise us about the Holy Spirit.

What should be the result of our embracing this promise?

_____

If, after you've tried, you'd like to see my answers, turn to page 106.

Many books have been written about how to have a successful Christian life, but success as a Christian really boils down to one primary key: obedience. If we will live in obedience to God—aligning our lives with Scripture's truth—we will both avoid many of life's potholes and enjoy an intimate relationship with God.

Obedience doesn't guarantee that we will not experience difficulty and pain; in fact, God has made it clear we can expect challenges in life.

However, when we live in obedience to Him, we will be able to discover joy in the midst of all circumstances. We will experience His hand on our lives and will learn to acknowledge His perspective on our circumstances.

John 14:26 promises that the Holy Spirit will be our teacher. He will not only *reveal* the truth to us as we study God's Word, He also will *remind* us of the truth as we apply it to our real-life situations. Because of this promise, I can have peace that God is going to give me all that I need to understand Scripture and to apply it to my life.

As we begin our look at Philippians, please understand that Bible study is not a passive process in which you just sit back and wait for God to hand you understanding without effort on your part! Bible study requires action—a willingness to spend time in God's Word and an open heart to hear His voice.

Read 2 Timothy 2:15.

To help you correctly handle the Word, I am going to introduce you to some tools that will help you unwrap beautiful nuggets of truth. Together let's explore the Bible: that most wonderful, life-changing Book!

Question Tool

Asking questions is a very helpful tool in studying the Bible. Begin by asking some very basic questions: Who?, What?, When?, Why?, Where?, and How? Then later, using a little imagination, you can create dozens of questions using these six basic questions as question-starters.

Read Philippians 1:1-11 and apply the Question Tool.

Who was writing this letter (v. 1)?_____

Who was it written to (v. 1)?_____

Where was this letter being sent (v. 1)?_____

_____

How did the letter writer feel about these people (vv. 3-4)?

_____

Why did Paul feel this way about them (vv. 5-8)?

_____

What was he sure of (v. 6)?

_____

What did Paul pray for (v. 9)?

_____

Why did he pray this prayer (vv. 10-11)?

_____

For a while, I'll share my answers with you. Be sure to complete the activity before checking pages 106–107.

When I was in high school, I took the Scholastic Aptitude Test (SAT). Part of that test was designed to assess reading comprehension. After reading a brief article, I was to answer a series of questions to see how much information I had absorbed. I was amazed to see how much I had overlooked!

When we study the Bible, we sometimes fail to process what we are reading. Going back and answering some basic questions helps us note the details in a passage so that we won't miss the important principles God communicates to us through Scripture.

How's It Going?

Did you find the Question Tool easy to use? Finding answers to basic questions is often simple to accomplish, and I find that the Question Tool helps me slow down and really note the details of what I am reading.

Application Tool

Application is another important key to studying the Bible. Always end your study time by summarizing each passage so that you walk away with a good grasp of what you have read, or the "bottom line." Your goal is to answer these questions: "What does God want me to learn from this passage?" and "How does this passage apply to my life?"

In some cases, committing a verse to memory helps you make application. Ask yourself: *Is there a verse I might memorize to help me remember what I learned?*

Let's summarize what we studied today and then take a look at how it applies: Philippians 1:1-11 paints a picture of partners working together to accomplish God's purposes *(summary)*. When we work together toward a common goal, we often discover joy, comradery, and a sense of purpose *(application)*.

A team of eight ladies leads women's ministry at Fellowship Church, in Grapevine, Texas, where I serve. I have the privilege of coordinating their work. Though we have difficulties and challenges in our personal lives, we experience joy when we come together. As we spend time working and praying together, we discover joy because we are part of a team that strives toward a common goal. Like the early Christians who worked together to spread the gospel, we have come to love and appreciate each other as we spend time together in ministry.

Another application of Philippians 1:1-11, then, is to identify some partners in your spiritual walk. Are you part of a group that strengthens and encourages you as together you work toward a common goal? If so, pause to thank God for that group.

If not, list some of your interests below. Ask God to bring into your life people who share those interests and who might become a source of spiritual support.

1. _____

2. _____

3. _____

4. _____

Don't allow yourself to become isolated. God wants to use the people around you to strengthen and encourage you.

In Psalm 119:11 the writer states, "I have treasured Your word in my heart so that I may not sin against You." This verse reminds me of another important part of application: memorization. Each of us should begin to memorize key verses so we can quickly recall them. I cannot tell you how many times God has brought a memorized verse to my mind just when I needed it!

Get in the habit of watching for verses that you can memorize so you can experience the heart-change God wants to bring to your life. A great verse from our passage for today might be: "I am sure of this, that He who started a good work in you will carry it on to completion until the day of Christ Jesus" (Phil. 1:6).

Write a verse from today's study that you would like to memorize:

_____

_____

I can't wait to see how God is going to finish what He has started in you!

Day 2 Seeing Life Through God's Eyes

Many scholars think Paul wrote the Book of Philippians while he was imprisoned in Rome. If you would like a little more background about the circumstances concerning how Paul came to be imprisoned, read chapters 25–28 in the Book of Acts.

Read Philippians 1:12-14.

Philippians 1:12-14

¹²Now I want you to know, brothers, that what has happened to me has actually resulted in the advancement of the gospel, ¹³so that it has become known throughout the whole imperial guard, and to everyone else, that my imprisonment is for Christ. ¹⁴Most of the brothers in the Lord have gained confidence from my imprisonment and dare even more to speak the message fearlessly.

Let's start today's study by asking our six key questions. I have given you a few to get started (Who?, What?, Why?), but feel free to add your own.

Who is this passage about?

_____

What has happened to Paul?

_____

What are the results of Paul's imprisonment?

_____

Why were others encouraged to preach more courageously?

_____

If you'd like to see my answers after writing yours, turn to page 107.

What additional questions would you ask?

_____

_____

Paul had a gift for seeing his life through God's eyes. He didn't allow pain and suffering to defeat him or to take his focus off of the priority of spreading the gospel message. Instead, he took time to ask, "How is God using this circumstance? What can I do or learn to help me carry out God's purposes for my life?"

The focus of Paul's life wasn't on himself, it was on God.

List some of the difficult circumstances you face, no matter how trivial or overwhelming they may seem.

_____

_____

_____

How could God use these difficult circumstances to teach you?

_____

_____

_____

_____

How could God use difficult circumstances to make a difference in your world?

_____

_____

_____

_____

What is God teaching you about how to handle life's challenges?

_____

_____

_____

_____

As I see challenges through God's eyes, I find that I can experience joy in the midst of pain because He has promised: "All things work together for the good of those who love God: those who are called according to His purpose" (Rom. 8:28).

Ask God to help you see the challenges in your life through His eyes.

Day 3 Celebrating When God Is Working

I have always been competitive. I remember going home after kinder-garten and crying because I had lost a game of musical chairs! Whether in the classroom, on the volleyball court, or in my dating relationships, I was always very aware of whether or not I was "winning."

Competition can be a positive force that pushes us toward excellence or a destructive force if it brings out envy and jealousy. We must be careful not to allow competition to create a barrier between us and the people around us.

Make a list of the people with whom you feel competitive.

_____

_____

Keep this list in mind. We'll work with our personal responses at the end of today's study.

Read Philippians 1:15-18 and answer the following questions.

What **are the two types of people described in this passage (v. 15)?**

_____

_____

Those preaching out of good will were motivated by

_____ **(v. 16).**

What **was Paul appointed to defend (v. 16)?**
❏ **the prison guard** ❏ **the sacrifice** ❏ **the gospel** ❏ **the rivalry**

Those preaching out of envy and strife were motivated out of

_____ **(v. 17).**

How **did those not motivated by love hope to impact Paul (v. 17)?**

_____

In the midst of all that was happening in this competition, *what* was most important to Paul (v. 18)?

_____

Because of this focus, *how* did Paul respond to Christ's message being proclaimed (v. 18)?

_____

When you are finished, you may want to check my responses on page 107.

Creative Tool

Reading creatively is an important part of studying the Bible. I use the Creative Tool when I imagine what emotions the characters were feeling by considering the emotions I would feel in a similar situation. This process allows me to better grasp the lesson God is trying to teach me. I'm not suggesting you add or take away anything from the Scripture text, but placing yourself in the character's place can add meaning to the verse.

Imagine that you have been imprisoned for sharing your faith. You receive word that your arrest has inspired others to courageously spread the good news of Jesus. However, some people take pleasure in your imprisonment and spread the gospel to mock your faith and reputation.

What emotions would you probably feel in the same situation? (Check all that apply or add your own to the list.)
❑ envy ❑ optimism ❑ frustration ❑ disappointment
❑ excitement ❑ anger ❑ joy ❑ _____ ❑ _____

How do you think Paul felt?

_____

_____

_____

You just used the Creative Tool to get your answers. Congratulations! In doing so, you tried to put yourself in Paul's shoes by attempting to experience his emotions and thoughts.

Like us, Paul was human. But he was not distracted by the competitiveness many of us would feel in this situation because his eyes were so clearly focused on Christ. Paul realized it was far more important for people to hear about Christ than to praise his own reputation or ministry.

Consider the following situations and check your most likely response:

When someone else receives the promotion that I wanted, I ...
❑ **feel jealous and make a mental list of why I am more qualified.**
❑ **talk to coworkers about the faults of someone newly-promoted.**
❑ **remember that God is in control and trust Him to work in my life.**

When another woman is praised for being a great mom, I ...
❑ **long to tell others about her yelling at her children in public.**
❑ **resent that no one equally recognizes my dedication to family.**
❑ **am thankful that God has given her children a good home.**

When someone else gets engaged and I am still single, I ...
❑ **say, "I'm so happy for you!" through gritted teeth.**
❑ **make a list of all the weddings I have attended in the last year.**
❑ **genuinely rejoice that God has given her someone.**

We often feel jealousy when others experience success. If we want to focus on Christ as Paul did, then we must remind ourselves that God's purposes, not our own, are most important. When we develop this kind of focus, we will experience joy in our relationship with Christ. At the same time, our relationships with other people will be closer to what God intended them to be.

Has God revealed jealousy or unhealthy competition in your life?
❑ **yes** ❑ **no**

Go back to your list of people with people with whom you feel competitive. How do you need to change your perspective?

_____

As you complete today's study, ask God to transform your heart so that you can truly rejoice when He works in the lives of others.

Day 4 Focusing on Heavenly Things

Paul had an exceptional ability to see his life through God's eyes. When he faced trouble, he saw it as an opportunity; when he faced competition, he focused on the end results. Today, we will analyze Paul's perspective regarding a life-or-death situation.

Read Philippians 1:19-26.

Use the six basic question-starters to create questions that will help you remember the details of this passage. Then answer your own questions.

Who? _____

_____

What? _____

_____

When? _____

_____

Why? _____

_____

Where? _____

_____

How? _____

_____

These were more difficult, weren't they? But you've had enough practice to find some of the details of this passage on your own. It may help to compare your thoughts with my questions and answers on pages 107–108. Remember, in this case, there are no right or wrong questions.

Paul loved the Philippian Christians. They had encouraged and prayed for him, and He was committed to investing himself in them. Though his love for them was deep, his love for Christ was much deeper. He longed to be with Christ in heaven. Paul saw living as an opportunity to serve God and dying as an opportunity to see God.

To understand Paul's perspective on life and death, consider these questions:

Paul was not focused on whether he was going to live. *What* was he focused on instead (v. 20)?

How did Paul view death (v. 21)?

Scripture Tool

Another important tool in Bible exploration involves *looking at other verses in the Bible that relate to the subject or passage* you are studying. For example, verses in other books of the Bible that describe joy will enrich our study of Philippians.

The Bible is meant to be studied as a whole, and the Scripture Tool helps. Using the entire Bible to research a topic will keep us from distorting the Truth.

Using the Scripture Tool and other Bible study tools may feel a little bit clumsy at first, but don't give up! You will become more comfortable with practice.

For a while, as in the following activity, I will give you verses to help familiarize you with how the Scripture Tool works. Later, when we learn to use the Resource Tool, you will be able to locate verses on your own.

Use the Scripture Tool to gain insight into verses 20-21. When I began thinking about Paul's perspective on life and death, I started to think about heaven. I wondered how the Bible describes heaven and wanted to know what verses throughout the Bible say about it.

Look up the following Scripture passages and list some of the things followers of Christ will gain when they die. (Hint: If you are unsure where to locate one of the books, see the alphabetical listing in the front of your Bible.)

John 14:2 _____

_____

2 Corinthians 4:17 _____

_____

Philippians 3:20-21 _____

_____

Revelation 7:16-17 _____

_____

Revelation 21:1-4 _____

_____

_____

Revelation 22:1-5 _____

_____

Since this is the first time we've used the Scripture Tool, you may want to compare your answers with mine on page 108.

What did Paul see as his purpose for remaining on earth (Phil.1:25-26)?

_____

_____

_____

Paul's perspective on death is probably one of the more difficult for me to apply. Frankly, I like being alive! I enjoy my life—it's not perfect and it has its share of challenges—but I still like it.

Last year my uncle was diagnosed with terminal cancer. Within a year, he went to be with the Lord—six months before his 50th birthday. He will never get to see his children get married. He will never be able to enjoy retirement with his wife.

During his final year with us, our family experienced not only times of sadness and tears but also times of laughter and hope. Although my uncle was realistic about his future, he was also focused on his purpose. His greatest desire was that in all things—even death—he would glorify God.

I have wondered many times what I would think in a similar situation. How would I respond to the news that I would die within months? I guess I can't really know the answers to those questions. But I can ask God to shape my heart so that I will one day be able to face death with the same dignity and focus that both Paul and my uncle demonstrated.

In Matthew 6:19-21 Jesus said:

"Don't collect for yourselves treasures on earth, where moth and rust destroy and where thieves break in and steal. But collect for yourselves treasures in heaven, where neither moth nor rust destroys, and where thieves don't break in and steal. For where your treasure is, there your heart will be also."

List the things that are most important to you—the things that would cause you the most stress if you were to lose everything. They may be either tangible or intangible things. You will not be asked to share this list, so be completely honest.

_____	_____
_____	_____
_____	_____
_____	_____

If we invest in earthly things—better jobs, bigger houses, nicer clothes, busier calendars—then our hearts will be focused on earthly things. If, instead, we focus on God's glory, God's purposes, and God's people— we will be focused on heavenly things. We will be able to experience joy even in the face of death. Close today's study by praying for God's focus.

Day 5 Standing with Christ

We started this week by discussing the value of walking through life with others who share our priorities and passions. Today we will look at the value of these relationships from a different perspective.

Read Philippians 1:27-30 and describe how you can live in a manner worthy of Christ ...

at home with family or roommates. _____

_____

at work. _____

_____

with friends in social situations. _____

_____

when dealing with conflict. _____

_____

when facing suffering. _____

_____

How's It Going?

What Bible study tool did you use? If you answered *Application Tool,* you are correct because you are personally applying Philippians 1:27-30.

Throughout Scripture, God gives us guidelines for how we are to live. In Philippians 1:27 Paul wrote that he wanted to hear that the believers were "standing firm in one spirit, with one mind, working side by side for the faith of the gospel." In other words, he wanted to hear that they were living in unity. Throughout the New Testament, we find that unity is one of the most distinctive qualities of the Christian life. Jesus also emphasized its importance. In John 17:20–21, He said,

> "I pray not only for these,
> but also for those who believe in Me
> through their message.
> May they all be one,
> as You, Father, are in Me and I am
> in You. May they also be one in Us,
> so that the world may believe You sent Me."

When we choose to be united, we reflect Jesus' relationship with God, the Father. Can you imagine Jesus saying to God, "You know, I really don't like Your plan. I love these people just like You do, but it just seems so unnecessary for Me to die for them! So, what do You say if I take some time to come up with some alternative plans and I'll get back with You? Or, if you prefer, You can just find someone else to do this job!" I am so glad Jesus modeled unity for us instead!

Read Luke 22:39-44 for an account of Jesus' actual conversation with the heavenly Father just before His crucifixion.

Jesus was not afraid to express His feelings to God openly in the garden of Gethsemane. However, He was always in complete unity with what God wanted—even when it meant submitting His will to the Father's.

When God commands believers to live in unity, He doesn't just expect us to get along with others when things are going well and when everyone is in agreement. He means for us to stand together when we are faced with opposition.

Why is unity so important for Christ-followers? Read the following verses and briefly describe what that Scripture says about unity.

Romans 15:5-6 _____

_____

1 Corinthians 1:10 _____

_____

Ephesians 4:3,13 _____

_____

Colossians 3:14 _____

_____

Paul points out that when we are united, we can all look toward a common goal without being distracted. Our common goal is to tell people around us about Jesus Christ. Because we stand with fellow believers and the Holy Spirit, we can do so without fear.

What emotions do you feel when you take a stand ...

in your neighborhood? _____

at work? _____

with family? _____

in your social circle? _____

Describe a time when you took a stand alone.

_____

_____

_____

How would you have felt differently if others had stood alongside you?

_____

_____

_____

If you have ever stood alone, you recognize the value of having others by your side. As believers, we find strength in our numbers as we choose to stand together for Christ. Instead of standing alone in fear, we can stand together with joy.

"Therefore, my dear brothers, be steadfast, immovable, always excelling in the Lord's work, knowing that your labor in the Lord is not in vain" (1 Cor. 15:58).

Ask God to ...
1. give you courage to stand firmly for Him in your world.
2. bring believers into your life who will stand alongside you.
3. use you to encourage others who are standing firmly for Christ.

We have covered several topics today. Look back through the topics to refresh your memory. Identify those with which you most closely relate, and take a few minutes to list the "bottom line."

_____

_____

_____

What is God teaching you through your study this week?

_____

_____

_____

_____

_____

One of the most loved passages in Scripture is part of next week's study. Philippians 2 is important because it is based on the humility and service of Jesus Christ. I'll be praying for you as you delve into this significant passage.

Cast like Christ

VIEWER GUIDE

TRANSFORMED RELATIONSHIPS BEGIN WITH TRANSFORMED INDIVIDUALS

Looking good on the outside is vastly different than allowing God to do the work of changing us from within. How does true transformation take place? (See Phil. 2:1-11.)

Keys to Being Transformed:

1. Recognize that I am _____ _____ to God.
   True change happens from the inside out.

2. Recognize that I am _____ by God.
   The only way I can completely trust God is when I know He loves me.

3. Recognize _____ I _____ God.
   When we obey God, we are choosing to realign our lives to His.

How are my relationships transformed? (See Phil. 2:14-15.)

Relationships are transformed by:

1. Changed _____

2. Changed _____

"Be blameless and pure, children of God who
are faultless in a crooked and perverted generation,
among whom you shine like stars in the world."
Philippians 2:15

THIS WEEK'S SCRIPTURE: PHILIPPIANS 2

Casting Versus Painting

When an object is cast in a color, it is literally made of that color. However, if an object is painted, it only displays a particular color on its surface. If the applied layer is scraped off a painted object, the completely different color underneath shows through.

As Christians we too often focus on how we should look on the outside, working hard to "play the game." But many of us stop short of allowing God to change our hearts, afraid of the hard work that He will do in our lives. Are you allowing Christ to cast you, transforming you from the inside out? Or is your relationship with Him only surface deep, as if it were painted on?

We must let God do the hard work required to change us from the inside out before we can experience the satisfying relationships He wants us to enjoy. In the second chapter of Philippians, Paul offers key qualities that should characterize our hearts if we are to experience relationships that bring us true joy. Paul's words remind me that a change in my relationships begins with a change in me.

A good way to check my progress as I allow God to cast my life is to see how I react to difficult relationships. Do I respond with patience, gentleness, and self-control? Or do I respond with a hot temper, sharp tongue, and cold intolerance?

This week continue to practice using the Bible study tools and allow God to transform your life as you apply what you learn. Remember that the purpose of studying Scripture is not only to add to your collection of Bible knowledge but also to learn more about God and His plan for your life. Ask Him to reveal areas in your heart that He wants to reshape so that you can experience a real change in your relationships.

Day 1 Practicing Humility

Before we get started, let's review some of the Bible study tools we learned to use last week.

1. Question Tool

Use the key questions "Who?, What?, When?, Why?, Where?, and How?" to help unlock the details of the passage.

2. Application Tool

Summarize what you have studied, and try to answer the questions: "What does God want me to learn from this passage?," "How does this apply to my life?," and "Is there a verse I might memorize to help me remember what I learned in this passage?"

3. Creative Tool

Explore the characters' emotions and circumstances. Consider the possibilities that will help you apply the passage to your life.

4. Scripture Tool

Other verses related to your topic shed new light on the passage you are studying and help you to see the full picture.

Read Philippians 2:1-4.

Philippians 2:1-4

[1]If then there is any encouragement in Christ, if any consolation of love, if any fellowship with the Spirit, if any affection and mercy, [2]fulfill my joy by thinking the same way, having the same love, sharing the same feelings, focusing on one goal. [3]Do nothing out of rivalry or conceit, but in humility consider others as more important than yourselves. [4]Everyone should look out not [only] for his own interests, but also for the interests of others.

Start with these key questions to discover the details in these verses. Feel free to add more of your own:

Whom **does Paul address here?** _____

What **benefits had the Philippians experienced as a result of their relationship with God (v. 1)?** _____

_____

What would make Paul's joy complete (v. 2)?

_____

What four factors in verse 2 work together to unify believers?

_____

_____

What does Paul contrast with humility in verse 3?

_____

How does Paul describe humility in verses 3 and 4?

_____

_____

What is a key attitude to living in unity with others?

_____

What does Paul mean when he mentions "thinking the same way"? Does he mean we must all have the same opinions and must literally see things exactly the same way?

❑ yes ❑ no Explain: _____

_____

Define the following in your own words:

rivalry: _____

conceit: _____

What additional questions would you ask?

_____

_____

How's It Going?

Which of the Bible study tools did you use to answer these questions? If you answered *Question Tool*, you are correct. You'll be surprised how many details you'll discover in Scripture by using this tool.

Living in unity does not mean that we become clones of one another—sharing the same feelings, opinions, and plans. Neither does it mean that we are to put ourselves down and act as if we are worthless. Instead, living in unity means that we stop pushing our own agendas and actively value the ideas and opinions of others. We become willing to set aside unimportant personal differences so that we can accomplish important godly goals.

For example, Fellowship Church began in 1990 with only 150 people attending. (Today more than 18,000 attend weekly worship services.) As you can imagine, this small group had a lot of work to do and many people to reach. Individuals who were a part of this early group had to remember one very important thing: they were working as a team toward one common goal—reaching the world for Jesus Christ. That often meant putting aside individual preferences and opinions to fulfill the vision God had given the leaders of Fellowship Church.

This committed group of people pulled together and started a ministry that eventually impacted people and churches locally and internationally. From local, national, and global projects, Fellowship Church reaches out to a world in need.

Are you fighting to get your own way in any area of your life?
❑ **yes** ❑ **no If yes, how is the fighting causing division?**

_____

_____

_____

Which of the following statements best describes your reaction
to opinions and ideas that are different from your own?
- ❏ I usually consider other opinions.
- ❏ I am usually critical of other opinions.
- ❏ I seldom ask others' opinions and make the decisions myself.
- ❏ Other:_____

Using the Application Tool, summarize today's study by listing the
"bottom line" lessons God wants to teach you from Philippians 2:1-4.

_____

_____

_____

_____

_____

As you conclude today's study, consider whether you have relationships
in which you do not display humility and unity. List two or more in
the space provided, and ask God to work in these areas. (We'll study
more about humility on day 2.)

_____

_____

_____

_____

_____

Ask God to teach you to reflect Him in these areas of your life.

Day 2 The Example of Humility

Today we continue our study of what it means to be humble by examining the ultimate example of humility: Jesus Christ. Today's study is based on Philippians 2:5-11. We will learn to use a new tool to explore its depths.

Relationship Tool

When we study Scripture, the Relationship Tool helps us *note elements that are contrasted and compared*. Biblical writers were inspired by the Holy Spirit to contrast different elements using words such as "but," "however," "or," and "instead." When they compare elements using words such as "and," "also," and "so then," they show us similarities.

Read Philippians 2:5-11, underlining its contrasts and comparisons.

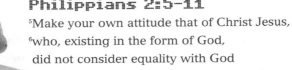

Philippians 2:5-11

[5]Make your own attitude that of Christ Jesus,
[6]who, existing in the form of God,
did not consider equality with God
as something to be used for His own advantage.
[7]Instead He emptied Himself by assuming the form of a slave,
taking on the likeness of men.
And when He had come as a man in His external form,
[8]He humbled Himself by becoming obedient
to the point of death—even to death on a cross.
[9]For this reason God also highly exalted Him
and gave Him the name that is above every name,
[10]so that at the name of Jesus every knee should bow—
of those who are in heaven and on earth and under the earth—
[11]and every tongue should confess that Jesus Christ is Lord,
to the glory of God the Father.

What is compared in verse 5?

_____

What does the contrast in verses 6-7 tell us about Christ's nature?

_____

What qualities are used to describe Christ in verse 7?

_____

This comparison continues into verse 8, with the word "even" indicating a continuing comparison. What were the results of Jesus' humbling Himself?

_____

Since this is the first time we've used the Relationship Tool, you may want to compare your answers to mine on pages 108–109.

Jesus made the choice to come to earth as a human. Though He was still God, He took on the limitations of a human body. In appearance, attitude, and action, He reflected how we should live as human followers of God.
- We are to recognize that we are not equal to God.
- We are to be humble before God.
- We are to be obedient to God.

The first step to developing a humble heart is to recognize that we don't deserve to be in charge. Such authority is God's exclusive right. Each of us must acknowledge that we are less than God in every way.

When I accept that God is in charge and stop struggling to control my own life, I am humbled before God. I don't stand before Him with arrogance, as if I know what is best, or with presumption, as if I have a right to call the shots. Instead, I humbly present myself to God as a servant who carries out His purposes.

When willing to serve God, I respond to Him in obedience. You see, my disobedience to God is more than committing sins or making bad choices. My disobedience takes God off the throne in my life and seats me in His place. By disobeying His commands, I choose to be in charge—ignoring God's rightful place in my life.

My actions are one of the clearest indicators as to whether I have the right attitude. If I have an attitude of humility before God, then I will live a life of obedience to Him.

What do your actions say about the condition of your heart?
❏ I struggle with obedience. ❏ Obedience is a pattern of my life.
❏ Other: _____

Thank God for transforming your heart into the heart of a servant, or ask Him to start the transformation as you make the decision to live in obedience to Him.

Cause-and-effect, another part of the Relationship Tool, is also helpful when studying the Bible. This relationship is often indicated by such words as "if," "then," "so," and "therefore."

Reread Philippians 2:9-11.

What word in this passage indicates a cause-and-effect relationship?

_____

What cause-and-effect relationship is described?

_____

_____

Jesus' life did not end with His being humbled as a servant. Instead, it continues with His being exalted as King. God's ultimate purpose in all things—even Jesus' pain and suffering on the cross—is that He will be glorified and worshiped. Every knee will bow and every tongue will confess Christ in heaven and on earth.

True joy does not come from being in charge; it comes from humbly acknowledging that God is in control. Joy is a product of worshiping the only One worthy of our praise and humbly serving Him in every aspect of our lives. When we obediently serve God, we carry out the purposes for which we were created. When we fulfill God's purposes, we experience true joy.

Day 3 Trusting by Faith

As a child, I quickly learned that I needed to obey my parents to avoid punishment. However, I also learned obedience was primarily important when my parents were present. Since obedience was little more than a way to avoid scolding, I felt no motivation to do the right thing when they were not around. I knew better than to hit my brother when they were in the room, but if they weren't in the room …

As years passed and I developed a stronger love and respect for my parents, my motivation changed. I wanted to be obedient to them because I knew it was the right thing to do—whether or not they were present. Obedience was no longer about avoiding punishment; it was about showing my parents my love and respect. True obedience changed more than just my outward actions; it changed the attitude of my heart.

Right motives make a difference in my attitude as an adult as well. If I make dinner because I know my husband expects it or because I'm afraid his empty stomach will make him grouchy, then I experience drudgery as I mash the potatoes and season the roast. But if I make dinner because I love my husband and know he will appreciate it, the tasks bring me joy.

Today we will take a brief look at why we are to be obedient, exploring how true obedience can bring us joy.

Read Philippians 2:12-13.

Using the tools we have learned, record appropriate information from Philippians 2:12-13 in the spaces provided. Make note of any questions that may require further study.

Question Tool (Details Matter)
Use questions to find the details of Philippians 2:12-13.

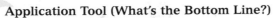

Application Tool (What's the Bottom Line?)

Ask yourself: *What does God want me to learn from this passage?*

Creative Tool (Imagine the Emotions)

What do you think the Philippians felt upon hearing the words, "work out your own salvation with fear and trembling"?

Scripture Tool (Other Verses Help)

What *words* or *topics* might help you find other verses that could shed more light on verses 12-13?

Relationship Tool (The Three C's)
Note any comparisons, contrasts, or cause-and-effect outcomes.

You may want to compare your responses to mine on page 109.

The full implications of the admonition to "work out your own salvation" are challenging for many believers. Some believe that Jesus came to give them life, but now it is up to them to live to the best of their abilities. I meet many people who have grown up in church or who have been Christ-followers for a long time, and a number of them are exhausted from trying to be good.

Let's see what the Bible has to say about that tendency. Even if these verses seem familiar to you, read them carefully so that you can clearly see what God wants to teach you about the spiritual truth we are unpacking from Philippians.

Read Romans 3:23 and Romans 6:23.

These verses make it clear that we are all sinners; we all deserve to die because of our sins.

Read Ephesians 2:8-10.

Because of our sin, we all deserve death. However, we can be saved from this death through faith in Jesus Christ.

With *what* is faith contrasted in these verses?

_____

What does Ephesians 2:10 tell us about our life purpose?

_____

True, we are to do good works as we live in obedience to Christ; however, we don't do works so that we will be saved. Ephesians 2:8 makes it clear that we are saved through faith, and then we obediently do the good works that God prepares for us. Unfortunately, many of us believe that while we can rely on God to save us from our sin, we must rely on ourselves to live obediently.

Read Romans 1:16-17 below:

[16]I am not ashamed of the gospel, because it is God's power for salvation to everyone who believes, first to the Jew, and also to the Greek. [17]For in it God's righteousness is revealed from faith to faith, just as it is written: The righteous will live by faith.

In verse 16, we see again that the gospel is _____'s power to save us.

How would you explain the relationship between faith and righteousness to a friend?

_____

When we choose to accept Jesus Christ as our Savior, we are declared "righteous." This word means that we become right with God when we accept Jesus into our hearts and lives. When God looks at us, He no longer sees the unpaid debt of our sins. Instead, He sees that Jesus paid the debt when He died for us. Because of that payment, we can have a personal relationship with Him.

If you have not yet accepted Jesus as your Savior, see page 105 for steps to becoming right with Him today.

Read Romans 1:17 again, and fill in the blanks:

"The _____ will live by _____."

This phrase helps us make an important connection. We are not only saved by faith, we also live by faith. We are not only declared righteous by faith, we also live righteous lives by faith. We must completely depend on Jesus for salvation—we can do nothing to earn it.

Read Philippians 2:12 again. What do you think Paul meant by "work out your own salvation"?

_____

_____

_____

The verses we have studied make it clear that salvation is through faith in Jesus Christ and not through our own good works. So we know that when Paul said to "work out your own salvation" that he didn't mean that we must work for salvation.

Many of us think that salvation—forming a relationship with Jesus Christ through faith—is the end goal. In reality, accepting Jesus is only the beginning of the journey. Our lifelong goal is to bring glory and honor to God in all that we do.

How can we bring glory and honor to God (Phil. 2:13)?

_____

_____

_____

When Paul tells us to work out our salvation, he is telling us to finish what God started at the time of our salvation. God is the source of our salvation, and He supplies us with the power and desire to serve Him. By faith we trust that God can work in us to carry out His purposes.

God often works through me when I pray, "God, I know what I should do, but I don't have the strength or desire to do it. Please change my heart so that I will desire what You desire. In the meantime, give me the strength to do what You want me to do. Thank You for not making me walk life's road alone!"

How do I find joy in obedience? By being obedient because of love rather than obligation. By depending on God to help me be obedient rather than depending on my own efforts. Ask God to show you when you are obedient for the wrong reasons or are trying to be obedient in your own efforts.

Day 4 Serving God

Sometimes I wish Paul had been a little less direct! When you read today's Scripture, you will see what I mean.

Read Philippians 2:14-18.

According to these verses, when is it acceptable for believers to complain or argue?

_____

Organization Tool

The process of _organizing facts and information_ is a helpful tool in studying the Bible. When you read a passage, make lists or draw diagrams to help organize the details. Be creative so that you can clearly see the picture God is describing for you!

Make a list of the qualities that define followers of Christ.

By contrast, how does Paul describe the world (v. 15)?

_____

Use the following space to draw a picture illustrating verses 14-16. Have fun and don't be shy!

In verses 14-16, Paul paints a beautiful picture of our purity and unity shining brilliantly in a dark world. List some examples of how we, as followers of Christ, "shine like stars."

_____

_____

What are some examples of how our "light" has been dimmed?

_____

_____

In verse 17, Paul compares his being poured out for Christ to the drink offering pictured in the Old Testament. See Numbers 28:1-8 to explore the comparison.

To what is Paul comparing the Philippians' service (v.17)?

_____

Elsewhere, Paul tells us to "present your bodies as a living sacrifice, holy and pleasing to God; this is your spiritual worship" (Rom. 12:1-2). Paul views the Philippians' service to God as a pleasing sacrifice. He would receive great joy even if his very life needed to be completely poured out for them—like a drink offering poured over a sacrifice.

In Paul's view, no sacrifice was too great. In fact, Paul considered giving his life for God to be the ultimate source of joy. Even as I write, our country is at war. As I see the faces of men and women who are willing to risk their lives to protect our country, I realize they have decided that no sacrifice is too great for the country they love.

As much as we love our country and are willing to serve and protect its citizens, our ultimate obligation is to Christ. What sacrifice are you willing to make for your Savior?

Day 5 Trusting Others

How wonderful to have people around us whom we can trust completely. Think of a close, trusted friend.

Describe how you feel when you think about that friendship.

_____

How would you feel if that friend were no longer a part of your life?

_____

Read Philippians 2:19-24.

Why did Paul trust Timothy so completely?

_____

Read Philippians 2:25-30.

Why did Paul commend Epaphroditus so highly?

_____

I don't think it is a coincidence that Philippians—this book about joy— is filled with references to friends who brought Paul joy. He admired Timothy's compassion and faithfulness. He also thanked God for Epaphroditus' service and commitment.

Let's explore more qualities of strong friendship.

What friendship qualities are described or implied in the following?

Proverbs 16:28 _____

Proverbs 17:9 _____

Proverbs 17:17 _____

Proverbs 18:24 _____

Proverbs 27:10 _____

Proverbs 27:17 _____

Ecclesiastes 4:9-10 _____

John 15:13 _____

These verses reveal truths that we need to acknowledge in our friendships.

What qualities do you already demonstrate in your friendships?

_____

What qualities do you need to develop? _____

_____

Unity and humility are essential qualities of strong friendships. I will not be open to the loving correction of a trusted friend if I don't have an attitude of humility. Likewise, I will not have the perseverance to build long-lasting friendships if I am not committed to unity.

Ask God to give you practical opportunities to develop these qualities in the friendships He brings into your life. As you allow Him to teach you, you will experience the joy of trusted friends who will support and encourage you in times of weakness.

Treasured by God

VIEWER GUIDE

THE WAY I SEE MYSELF AFFECTS
HOW MUCH I THINK I AM WORTH

Paul's Measure of Himself

1. "Circumcised the eighth day"
2. "Of the nation of Israel"
3. "Of the tribe of Benjamin"
4. "A Hebrew born of Hebrews"
5. "As to the law, a Pharisee"
6. "As to zeal, persecuting the church"
7. "As to … righteousness … blameless"

How We Measure Ourselves

1. Our _____ —where we _____ _____
   We often look at family as a measure of who we are.

2. Our_____ —how we _____
   We often look at media for our standard.

3. Our _____ —what we _____ _____
   We often take on the burden of trying to be perfect.

4. Our _____ —what we _____
   We are often tempted to compare what we have to what others have.

5. Our _____ —what we _____
   We often measure our spirituality by how we relate to God.

> "Everything that was a gain to me, I have
> considered to be a loss because of Christ."
> *Philippians 3:7*

True Measure of Value

Do you ever just want to get away? Sometimes we feel that if we could just escape our lives for a few minutes, we could experience real joy. But escaping wouldn't really fix our problems because we are the real source of our unhappiness. The reason we are dissatisfied with life may be because we are dissatisfied with who we are. No matter how hard we try, we feel as if we can never quite measure up to the unreachable standards that constantly haunt us.

We listen to the world around us to determine whether we are good enough. But no matter how much we achieve, we will find that the pressure to be and stay on top is enough to wear out even the most dedicated over-achiever.

This week we will begin to look at the third chapter of Philippians. Here Paul notes the standards by which we measure our value. Then he helps us to gain a new perspective on what makes us valuable. As I studied this section of Philippians, I found that only when I understand how God views me do I finally find joy in who I was created to be.

As you use the study tools, you may find that some of them—depending on your personality and experience—are easier to use than others. Keep practicing—even with those tools you find difficult! The more you use the tools to examine Scripture and understand its meaning, the easier it will become to apply these passages to your daily life. And you are well on your way to experiencing the thirst-quenching satisfaction that comes from being able to read and understand Scripture for yourself.

Day 1 Avoiding Traps

Driving home from work and feeling pretty satisfied with the day, I got stuck behind a car that was going exactly three miles below the speed limit. I was amazed to see how quickly I became annoyed by the slow driver who had dared to drive in the left lane. In an instant, I allowed one insignificant circumstance to replace my joy with frustration.

Before we begin our study, take a few minutes to think back over this past week …

Have you experienced any challenging circumstances? ❑ yes ❑ no
If yes, have any of these situations replaced your joy with anger, worry, frustration, jealousy, or fear? ❑ yes ❑ no **Explain:**

_____

_____

_____

Have you encountered any relationships this week in which you experienced stress, conflict, or disappointment? ❑ yes ❑ no
If yes, explain:

_____

_____

_____

Always remember that we can feel these negative emotions and still experience joy. The reason? Joy is a hopeful peace that permeates our lives when we see our circumstances, our relationships, and our very selves through God's eyes. In contrast, negative emotions, when they result from a faulty perspective, often crowd out the joy in our lives.

During week 1 we learned that we are to view challenges, competition, and even life and death through God's eyes. In week 2 we learned we are to approach our relationships with an attitude of humility and service that will lead to unity and sacrifice.

In light of what you have learned, how could you change your response to the challenging situation you listed? How could you still experience joy in the midst of your other emotions? Be specific. It may be helpful to reread Philippians 1:1—2:30 before answering.

_____

_____

_____

_____

_____

As we study the Bible, we can easily fall into one of two traps: the "To Do Trap" or the "To Know Trap." When I do my Bible study so that I can check it off my "To Do" list rather than taking the time to truly absorb what God is wanting to teach me, I fall into the "To Do Trap." The "To Know Trap" ensnares me when I become focused on filling my head with Bible knowledge instead of applying God's truth to every area of my life.

In James 1:22-25, God warns us:

[22]Be doers of the word and not hearers only, deceiving yourselves. [23]Because if anyone is a hearer of the word and not a doer, he is like a man looking at his own face in a mirror; [24]for he looks at himself, goes away, and right away forgets what kind of man he was. [25]But the one who looks intently into the perfect law of freedom and perseveres in it, and is not a forgetful hearer but a doer who acts—this person will be blessed in what he does.

How's It Going?

Are you becoming more comfortable with the Bible study tools? Are they helping you unpack the wealth that is in Philippians? Remember, these are tools from which you can choose—except for the following new tool. You should use it every time you study the Bible.

Prayer Tool

One way to avoid both the "To Do Trap" and the "To Know Trap" is to begin and end each Bible study time with prayer. Begin by asking God to reveal to you the things you need to learn and to show you how to apply them to your life. As you read each passage, note truths that stand out to you. *Ask God for insight* and help in your Bible study time.

List ways you want to apply the principles you have learned to your life this week. Then pray about each one.

We would miss much of Paul's heart for ministry if we fail to recognize the importance he placed on prayer. It would prove to be especially needed as the early Christians struggled with some potentially divisive issues. You'll learn more about one issue in day 2 and 3.

Day 2 An Outward Symbol

Let's review the Bible study tools we've learned.

1. **Question Tool**
   Use the key questions "Who?, What?, When?, Why?, Where?, and How?" to help unlock the details of the passage.
2. **Application Tool**
   Summarize what you have studied. Try to answer these questions: "What does God want me to learn from this passage?" and "How does this apply to my life?" In some cases memorization will help you make application personal. Always ask yourself, *Is there a verse I might memorize to help me remember what I learned in this passage?*

3. **Creative Tool**

   Explore the characters' emotions and circumstances. Consider the
   possibilities that will help you apply the passage to your life.

4. **Scripture Tool**

   Use other verses related to your topic to shed new light on the passage
   you are studying and to help you see the full picture.

5. **Relationship Tool**

   Note any contrasts, comparisons, or cause-and-effect relationships
   within the Scripture.

6. **Organization Tool**

   Organize the details of a passage by making lists or drawing diagrams.

7. **Prayer Tool**

   Pray before, during, and after your time of Bible study.

**Use the Prayer Tool. Before you start your Bible study today, ask
God to give you insight and understanding as you study His Word.**

Today we will add a new tool that will help us to further explore the Book
of Philippians.

Resource Tool

The Resource Tool introduces us to *outside resources* such as concordances, dictionaries, and commentaries that can help us understand
unfamiliar terms and concepts.

We can often get a better feel for context as we compare the verses we
are studying with other Scriptures. *Concordances* are helpful in finding
related Scripture verses. We will look at two types today: the word
concordance and the topical concordance.

While most Bibles contain concordances, they are not always labeled
as word or topical. However, the two types function similarly. Generally,
a word concordance allows us to look up a specific word to find a list of
verses that contain that word. A topical concordance allows us to look
up a particular word or topic to find a list of verses that contain related
information. In a topical concordance, the related verses may not actually
mention the exact word you are researching, but they may give more
insight into the topic as a whole. Look in the back of your Bible to see
whether you have a concordance.

If you do not have these tools in the back of your Bible, you can purchase most of them in Christian book stores; or you may find them online. To use an online resource, try *www.lifeway.com* and choose the resource you want to use; or go to *www.crosswalk.com*. Click on "Bible Study Tools," and then enter the word or topic you want to find. See page 112 for more ideas.

Circle any words in Philippians 3:1-4 that are unfamiliar or about which you would like to learn more.

Philippians 3:1-4

¹Finally, my brothers, rejoice in the Lord. To write to you again about this is no trouble for me and is a protection for you. ²Watch out for "dogs," watch out for evil workers, watch out for those who mutilate the flesh. ³For we are the circumcision, the ones who serve by the Spirit of God, boast in Christ Jesus, and do not put confidence in the flesh—⁴although I once had confidence in the flesh too. If anyone else thinks he has grounds for confidence in the flesh, I have more.

The goal of the Resource Tool is to help us understand terms and concepts that seem unclear or confusing. No matter which terms you circled, you probably identified at least a few concepts that seemed difficult to understand.

For instance, the first time I read this passage, I realized I wasn't sure what Paul meant by "we are the circumcision." So I picked up my Bible and looked up the word *circumcision* in my concordance. I looked it up alphabetically—just as I would if I were looking it up in a dictionary. Under the term I discovered a long list of places in the Bible where circumcision is either practiced or discussed. In fact, my concordance offered variations of the word; in this case, the word *circumcise*.

For easier reference, concordances often give a short phrase explaining the content of each verse listed below a term. This helps you to decide which of the verses may prove most relevant to the passage you are studying. And sometimes, when many options are given, you will find the short phrases helpful in choosing which verses to view first.

Today we will use our concordances to understand the significance of circumcision. Since you may not have access to a concordance today, I will give you some of the verses that were listed under *circumcise* in my concordance.

Summarize what you learn about circumcision from these passages.

Genesis 17:1-14 _____

_____

_____

Deuteronomy 30:6 _____

_____

_____

Romans 2:28-29 _____

_____

_____

Galatians 6:12-16 _____

_____

_____

Colossians 2:11-12 _____

_____

_____

By researching the word *circumcision* with the help of my concordance, I discovered a number of things. First, circumcision was an outward evidence of the inward faith of Abraham and his descendants—the Jewish people. This practice was an expression of their belief that God would be faithful to fulfill His promises.

After Christ's death and resurrection, the special relationship that God had with the Jewish people was made available to the entire world—including the Gentiles (non-Jewish people). The relationship still came through faith, but it came specifically through faith in Jesus Christ. Anyone who believes that Jesus is the Son of God and that He came to give us eternal life through His death and resurrection can have a restored relationship with God.

Baptism is the outward evidence of this inward faith. Like circumcision, baptism is not required for salvation. We observe this practice in obedience to Jesus' command. Baptism presents a beautiful picture of Christ's death and resurrection as well as the death of our "old self" and the birth of our "new self."

Our "new self" is filled with the Holy Spirit. Just as the Jewish men in the Old Testament were physically marked through circumcision, so are we spiritually marked by the Holy Spirit when He comes to change our hearts. This is what Paul meant when he said "circumcision is of the heart" (also see Rom. 2:29).

Much debate surrounded the practice of circumcision and how it fit in with becoming a Christ-follower. Because circumcision was such an important part of the Jewish faith, some Jewish Christians had a difficult time not continuing the practice. Many believed that any Gentile who became a Christ-follower should also be circumcised. However, Paul argued that faith in Christ alone is enough for salvation. No other requirements need to be added.

The issue of whether circumcision was to be required was debated and resolved at the Jerusalem Council.

As you've probably already discovered, sometimes the search for answers to one question raises other questions! Take a moment to read Acts 15:1-11 for background on the Jerusalem Council.

Now that we have this information, we are better equipped to apply Paul's letter to our lives.

Reread Philippians 3:1-4, our focal passage for today, in light of your new understanding.

In verse 2, Paul refers to those who still think that Gentiles should be circumcised before they can be Christ-followers. He condemns them because they continue to follow their own agenda.

What verses in Philippians 3:1-4 describe the true heart motives of those who wanted to require circumcision?

_____

_____

Apply three tools to this passage to unpack the details.

Relationship Tool: _____

_____

_____

Organization Tool:_____

_____

_____

Application Tool: _____

_____

_____

After you've completed this activity, see how I used these tools on page 110.

We will continue to practically apply some of the concepts we have learned today. Close your study time by asking God to help you live as a Christ-follower who has been "marked" by the Holy Spirit.

Day 3 Inward Faith

Yesterday we looked at the history behind the practice of circumcision. We learned that circumcision was an outward, physical evidence of internal, spiritual faith.

We would all agree that inward, spiritual change is more important than outward symbols. However, because we can see outward, physical evidence more readily, we often get our priorities mixed up and focus more on the external.

Pray that God will open today's passage so that you will understand how He wants you to apply it to your life.

Read the following verses. Write any unfamiliar or unclear terms or names in the margin.

Philippians 3:3-6

³For we are the circumcision, the ones who serve by the Spirit of God, boast in Christ Jesus, and do not put confidence in the flesh—⁴although I once had confidence in the flesh too. If anyone else thinks he has grounds for confidence in the flesh, I have more: ⁵circumcised the eighth day; of the nation of Israel, of the tribe of Benjamin, a Hebrew born of Hebrews; as to the law, a Pharisee; ⁶as to zeal, persecuting the church; as to the righteousness that is in the law, blameless.

We will use our concordances again to try to understand these terms and names. I selected the following terms from today's passage and used my concordance to find Scriptures related to each concept. Because everyone is different, your choices probably differ from mine.

Read the following passages and write the details you discover.

Israel—Exodus 6:6-8 _____

_____

_____

Benjamin—Genesis 49:27-28 _____

_____

_____

Hebrew—Genesis 14:13 _____

_____

Zeal—Acts 26:9-11 and Galatians 1:13-14 _____

_____

_____

Bible dictionaries, which are available online and in Christian book stores, provide a different approach to understanding the terms and concepts within a passage. Unlike commentaries, Bible dictionaries do not always offer lists of references related to specific words or topics. However, they do give short descriptions, summaries, and basic information that help us grasp concepts. More importantly, Bible dictionaries usually define words within the context of Scripture.

For example, when we look up the word *Pharisee* in a Bible dictionary, we find that Pharisees appeared in the Gospels as opponents of Jesus. They controlled the synagogues and exercised great control over the general population. Their name means "the separated ones," which may be because they separated themselves from the masses to focus on the study and interpretation of the law. They saw obedience to the law as the way to God.

What did Paul mean when he said that he was a Pharisee (v. 5)?

_____

Look up another key term from Philippians 3:3-6: *flesh*. Use a Bible dictionary to gain a more complete understanding of its meaning in this context.

_____

_____

After you've looked it up, you may want to see my findings on page 110.

Organize the details of Philippians 3:3-6 by making lists or drawing diagrams.

Briefly summarize what you have studied today.

_____

_____

Enjoy

What does God want you to learn from this passage?

_____

_____

How does this knowledge apply to your life?

_____

_____

Tomorrow we will look at the outward credentials on which we often rely to measure our worth. Ask God to prepare you for what He wants to teach you about this common trap.

Day 4 Measuring Worth

On day 2 we studied circumcision, learning that it was an outward sign of inward faith for the Jewish people. After Christ's death, a debate ensued about whether circumcision should be required for salvation. Participants at the Jerusalem Council agreed that people can have a relationship with God through faith. Circumcision is not necessary, and no other actions need to be added.

Throughout his ministry, Paul battled against anyone who taught that salvation—a relationship with God—can be earned through human efforts and accomplishment.

On day 3 we learned Paul anticipated some would argue that those who wanted salvation to be through faith alone were those who were ashamed of their lives, knowing they could never earn salvation. So Paul started his argument by listing his own credentials. He made the point that if anyone could be called a "good Jew," he could. Paul came from a strong Jewish family and was well-educated in the Jewish faith; he had demonstrated his commitment and passion by persecuting anyone who opposed him; and he had lived a life above reproach. If anyone could claim to be a devout person, Paul could!

With this backdrop in mind, read Philippians 3:4-9.

Now make a list of the accomplishments and credentials of which you are most proud. No one else is going to see this list, so don't hold back!

_____

_____

_____

_____

What value did Paul place on accomplishments and credentials (v. 7)?

_____

Why did they no longer seem valuable (v. 8)?

_____

We often base our happiness on whether we feel successful. We feel pressure from others and from ourselves to prove our value.

What are some areas in which you feel you have to prove yourself?

_____

_____

Paul had set his priorities right. When he looked at his accomplishments through God's eyes, he suddenly saw their true value and understood that nothing was more valuable than his faith in Christ. Paul realized that if he did not believe in Christ and follow Him, nothing else mattered.

This week we have been studying this passage without mentioning joy. What does Philippians 3:4-9 have to do with finding joy?

_____

_____

_____

When we measure our worth by our accomplishments, we feel pressure to succeed and compete. There's nothing like a little pressure to rob us of joy! But I've found that when I realize that my accomplishments and credentials are rubbish compared to knowing Christ, then the pressure is off. I find my worth and my joy in Him, and I have no excuse to settle for mediocrity.

Success and accomplishments are not wrong. However, when they drive our lives, they rob us of the joy God intended us to experience in our relationship with Him.

In Philippians 3:8-9, Paul says,

> ⁸I also consider everything to be a loss in view of the surpassing value of knowing Christ Jesus my Lord. Because of Him I have suffered the loss of all things and consider them filth, so that I may gain Christ ⁹and be found in Him, not having a righteousness of my own from the law, but one that is through faith in Christ —the righteousness from God based on faith.

The icing on the cake is that I am not only freed from having to prove myself to others, but I am also freed from having to prove myself to God. I do not enter a right relationship with God because I'm good enough or because I observe the law. I enter a right relationship with God because I accept that Jesus loved me enough to die for me.

What do Romans 5:8 and Ephesians 3:16-19 tell you about God's love for you?

_____

_____

_____

_____

_____

_____

As you close today's session, thank God for His incredible love that frees us from having to prove ourselves so we can experience joy.

Day 5 Knowing God

Paul sets a standard for us. His overarching goal was to know Christ.

Read Philippians 3:10-11, and then list the three things Paul wants to know. Pray over these verses.

_____

_____

_____

What additional truths about knowing God do you find in the following verses?

Psalm 46:10 _____

_____

_____

Jeremiah 24:7 _____

_____

_____

1 John 2:3-6 _____

_____

_____

Paul wanted to have an intimate relationship with God; he wanted to experience God's power in his life. In Philippians 3:10, Paul wrote that he wanted to know the power of the resurrection. To better understand the incredible power he referenced, let's explore Jesus' resurrection.

Read Matthew 27:57—28:10.

Let's use the Creative Tool to apply Matthew 27:57—28:10 to our lives. Close your eyes and imagine this scene through the eyes of the guard at the tomb. How would you feel if you were him?

_____

_____

_____

_____

_____

_____

The Creative Tool we just used helps me to imagine what I would have done in similar circumstances. If I had been the guard, I would have had no doubt of God's awesome power. Not only did God have the power to heal the sick, give sight to the blind, and provide food for the hungry, but He also had the power to give life to the dead.

Paul said in Philippians 3:10 that he wanted to know "the power of His resurrection." In other words, he wanted to experience in his life the same power that raised Jesus from the dead.

Isn't it amazing to realize that the same power that resurrected Christ is available for us? Whenever we face seemingly insurmountable obstacles, we can still have joy because we know that the One who has the power to raise the dead is the One who is at work in our lives! Nothing is impossible for Him!

Paul continued, "I want to know … the fellowship of His sufferings" (v. 10). Paul wanted to know Christ so intimately that he would experience the same pain Christ felt as well as the same power He displayed.

When Mike and I got married, my brother officiated our wedding. During the ceremony, he explained that our "joys would be multiplied and sorrows shared." Mike and I recognized that as a married couple, we would share many joys. In fact, our joys would be multiplied because we would not only experience joy in our individual lives, but also we would each share the joy that the other was experiencing. Likewise, we recognized that we would also share suffering. Persons in an intimate relationship share the good along with the bad.

A few weeks ago, I experienced sadness through a difficult circumstance. Mike did not say, "I'm so sorry, honey! Hope you get to feeling better!" before walking away. Instead, he put his arms around me, comforted me, and shared in my suffering.

Those experiencing a true, intimate relationship will not only share each other's joys, they will also share each other's hurts. Do you have that kind of sharing relationship with Christ? Are you willing to experience some of the same suffering that He experienced, or are you in a relationship with Jesus only because of the blessings and assurance of heaven that you can get out of it?

God has promised that we can experience joy through our relationship with Him. However, He never promised that life would be easy. In fact, He assured us of just the opposite: "In the world you have suffering. Be courageous! I have conquered the world" (John 16:33).

I can have joy in the midst of suffering because of the hope I find in this verse. No matter what I face, I am sure that God can handle it. He is on my side; I will never be alone.

Look over the verses you studied this week and choose a verse to memorize. Write it in the space provided.

_____

_____

_____

_____

_____

Take a few minutes to pray as you finish your study for this week. Confess to God any areas of your life in which you do not have His perspective.

Thank God for His power in your life. Ask Him to give you a desire to know Him so intimately that you would willingly share in His suffering. Thank Him that, even in those yet-unknown circumstances, you will experience His life-sustaining joy.

Running the Race

VIEWER GUIDE

OUR GOAL IS TO KNOW CHRIST INTIMATELY AND PERFECTLY

1. _____ in the _____ of past accomplishments can take our eyes off the goal.

2. _____ under the _____ of past failures can take our eyes off the goal.

3. _____ _____ can take our eyes off the goal.

4. _____ _____ by earthly goals and interests can take our eyes off the goal.

> *"One thing I do: forgetting what is behind and reaching forward to what is ahead, I pursue as my goal the prize promised by God's heavenly call in Christ Jesus."*
> *Philippians 3:13-14*

THIS WEEK'S SCRIPTURE: PHILIPPIANS 3:12-4:3

Focused on the Goal

Have you ever watched a world-class race? The runners' eyes stay focused ahead as they look toward the finish line. They have an incredible ability to tune out the many distractions around them, keeping their eyes locked on their destination.

In the third chapter of Philippians, Paul uses this racing analogy to help us understand how to live the Christian life. Our journey with Christ is not made up of a collection of spiritual highs only. Instead, we walk with Him daily as we keep our eyes on the ultimate goal: experiencing Christ fully so we can know Him intimately, just as He knows us.

As we journey together this week, we will look at experiences from our past that may cause us to take our eyes off the finish line. Then we will look at present distractions that may be causing us to look all around. Finally, we are going to learn how to keep our eyes on our ultimate goal and to walk, even run, with Jesus into the future.

The key to experiencing joy day in and day out is to understand that each day is part of this journey. The lessons we learn today are essential for the experiences we will have tomorrow. As these lessons and experiences build on each other, we will find that we are walking more closely to our teacher, Jesus Christ.

Walking with Him will be like walking with a best friend. Together we will build a history that will lead us into the future: a future that culminates when we reach our final destination—heaven. There we will see our Savior face-to-face.

Sometimes studying the Bible reminds me of reading a letter from a dear friend. I examine each word and try to understand its meaning. I take the message to heart and often walk away deeply touched and changed by the love found there.

I hope that you are catching a thirst-quenching glimpse of God's love for you as you apply His life-changing perspective to your own life.

Day 1 Moving Forward

It's time to review. Use the adjacent chart and your own memory and experiences with the tools to fill in the following blanks.

1. **Question Tool**—Use the six key _____ to help unlock the _____ of the passage.

2. **Application Tool**— _____ what you have studied. Try to answer these questions: "What does God want me to _____ from this passage?" "How does this _____ to my life?" "Is there a verse I might _____?"

3. **Creative Tool**—Look at the passage _____ to apply it to your life. Explore the characters' _____ and circumstances. Consider the possibilities that will help you apply the passage to your life.

4. **Scripture Tool**—Study other _____ that relate to the same topic, allowing God to speak to you in yet another way.

5. **Relationship Tool**—Note any _____, _____, or _____-and-_____ relationships within the Scripture.

6. **Organization Tool**—Organize the _____ of a passage by making _____ or drawing diagrams.

7. **Prayer Tool**— _____ before, during, and after your time of Bible study.

8. **Resource Tool**—Consult outside _____ to gather more information.

You may check your answers on page 111.

Read Philippians 3:1-11 to refresh your memory of what you studied last week. What are some key principles you learned in week 3 that you are applying to your life?

_____

_____

Now you're ready to read Philippians 3:12, our focal verse for today.

Philippians 3:12

Not that I have already reached [the goal] or am already
fully mature, but I make every effort to take hold of it
because I have also been taken hold of by Christ Jesus.

**Choose from the following to draw out the details of Philippians 3:12.
I'll let you know which ones I chose and what information I gained
by using them. But don't peek until you finish your work.**

Question Tool	Answer key questions to discover details.
Application Tool	Summarize the passage and attempt to discover what God would have you learn and apply to your life.
Creative Tool	Use your imagination to understand the emotions of the characters.
Scripture Tool	Study other verses that relate to the verse or topic.
Relationship Tool	Observe comparisons, contrasts, and cause-and-effect relationships within a passage.
Organization Tool	Organize details by making lists and drawing diagrams.
Prayer Tool	Permeate Bible study with prayer.
Resource Tool	Use outside resources such as concordances, dictionaries, and commentaries to understand unfamiliar terms and concepts.

_____

_____

_____

_____

_____

Circle the tools you used to get your details.

Your answers may differ from mine, but that's OK. As I selected tools and applied them to this passage, I made note of the following details:

What was Paul referring to when he said "Not that I have already reached [the goal]," at the beginning of verse 12? *(Question Tool)*

Paul was referring back to verses 10-11 where he described his desire to know Christ, the power of Christ's resurrection, and the fellowship of sharing in His suffering. While Paul desired to have an intimate relationship with Christ, he acknowledged that he was still working toward the goal. He had yet to obtain that level of maturity.

A *comparison* is made between reaching for the goal and already being fully mature *(Relationship Tool, Scripture Tool)*.

My Bible included a note in the margin to look at James 3:2 for another verse about our struggle toward maturity: "We all stumble in many ways. If anyone does not stumble in what he says, he is a mature man who is able to control his whole body."

James 3:2, then, clarifies Paul's comparison in Philippians between reaching for the goal and being fully mature. The James verse gives a different image of what maturity means for Christians who seek it but still stumble.

Paul went on to acknowledge that this kind of intimacy with Christ would never be obtained in his lifetime, just as we will never be completely mature in our lifetime. Though we may experience moments when we see things through God's eyes, experience His power, or suffer for Him, we will not have complete intimacy with Him until we are fully mature. Paul reminds us that maturity will not be reached until heaven.

The word "but" indicates contrast *(Relationship Tool)*.

Verse 12 contrasts Paul's past and his future. Even though he was not perfect, Paul made "every effort to take hold of" a future goal.

What does Paul want to "take hold of"? *(Question Tool)*

Paul wanted to take hold of the goal that Christ has for us—knowing Him intimately and glorifying Him in all that we do. Paul did not allow his shortcomings to discourage him. Instead, he kept reaching toward his goal of being more like Christ.

What does it mean to "take hold of"? *What* image does "press on" (NIV) bring to mind? *(Question Tool, Application Tool)*

While "take hold of" highlights an extra measure of persistence, "press on" also generates a helpful word picture. (While we've not talked about different Bible translations, reading different translations can add to our insights about a particular passage, as is true with the NIV translation of Phil. 3:12.)

When I think about the words "press on," I picture a long line of weary travelers. They know their destination, but it seems far away. Even so, they are in pursuit of their goal, pressing forward, always moving closer to their goal.

How would I summarize Philippians 3:12? *(Application Tool)*

Paul was encouraging the Philippians (and us) to keep moving forward. He spoke to them—not as someone who has already reached the goal—but as a fellow traveler. Paul's goal was to have an intimate relationship with God that completely transformed his perspective and his heart.

What does God want me to learn from this verse? *(Application Tool)*

Personally, I realized I must never become satisfied with how I have grown in my relationship with Christ. I must keep reaching forward to the ultimate goal of perfect intimacy, looking forward to the day when I will experience the fullness of that relationship in heaven.

I hope that you too will never become satisfied with your growth in your relationship with Christ. Instead, keep pressing forward to the ultimate goal of perfect intimacy, looking forward to the day you will experience that perfection in heaven.

How can I apply this verse to my life? *(Application Tool)*

From this passage, I learned the importance of not comparing myself to others and not resting on the laurels of past achievements. Instead, I want to continue to move forward in my relationship with Christ through daily obedience to Him.

How's It Going?

How did you do? Were you able to glean the details of Philippians 3:12 from your choice of Bible study tools? Which tool are you most comfortable with and why?

If you have not already done so, answer the following questions.

What does God want you to learn from Philippians 3:12?

_____

_____

_____

How can you apply this verse to your life?

_____

_____

_____

End your study time by using your Prayer Tool. List specific concerns that you need to pray about this week so that you can begin to apply what you are learning.

_____

_____

_____

_____

Philippians 3:12 should be a reminder to neither compare yourself with others nor rest on past accomplishments. Instead, continue to move ahead in your relationship with Christ through daily obedience to Him—with the same energy and devotion by which Christ Jesus has taken hold of you.

Close your study time today in prayer. Ask God to strengthen your obedience and your pursuit of this goal toward maturity.

Day 2 Overcoming Obstacles

Today we will work on combining several tools as we study our focal verses. Our passage today is great for using the Question, Scripture, and Resource Tools together. Let me show you what I mean ...

Read Philippians 3:13-14.

Let's start with the Question Tool to slow down and really think through the details of these two verses.

> **In verse 13, for instance, what does Paul mean by "it" when he says, "I do not consider myself yet to have taken hold of it"? Let's answer the question by using the Scripture Tool. Look back at Philippians 3:7-12, focusing on verse 10. Identify what Paul intends by referring to the word "it."**

_____

> **Now for another question: What are some parts of Paul's past that he had to forget? List some of your discoveries below.**

_____

_____

_____

_____

If you're not familiar with Paul's past, you will need to use the Resource Tool to answer this question. If you look up "Paul" in a word concordance, you'll likely find passages that tell about Paul as well as the persecutions that he endured.

What goal is Paul pursuing? _____

After I used the Question Tool to generate this question, I used the Scripture Tool to look back at another verse in chapter 3 in which Paul also referred to a "goal."

How does verse 10 describe Paul's goal?

_____

_____

Now let's see how we can connect this passage to our lives: The key to experiencing joy in our lives is in nurturing an intimate relationship with God. As we grow in our relationship with Him, He changes our perspective, desires, and attitudes. Unfortunately, this process is often derailed when we focus on our past.

Read the accomplishments and credentials you listed on day 4 of week 3 (p. 59). How can focusing on these accomplishments keep you from taking hold of the goal?

_____

_____

What are some of your failures and past sins? (You won't be asked to share your answers.)

_____

How can focusing on these failures and sins keep you from "pursuing the goal"?

_____

Imagine ... Scenario 1:
You are on the starting block, ready to compete for an Olympic gold medal in the 100-meter freestyle race. The gun fires, but you are so busy bragging to the crowd about all the competitions you have won that you are left behind. What are the chances that you will reach your goal?

When we rest on our past accomplishments, we are distracted from finishing the race. We settle for what we have already accomplished instead of pursuing the incredible goal that is still before us.

Imagine ... Scenario 2:
You are standing at the starting line, ready to compete for an Olympic gold medal in the 1-mile run. The gun fires and you take off—only to

discover that a 20-pound bag strapped to your left ankle is dragging behind you. What are the chances that you will reach your goal?

When we focus on our past failures, we are distracted from finishing the race. We convince ourselves that we have been disqualified and don't deserve the prize that is still ahead.

What distracts you from reaching toward the prize?

_____

_____

Prayerfully ask God to reveal your distractions and to redirect your focus on the future.

Day 3 Journey Travelers

When I was growing up, my family went on long vacations. Since we traveled on a budget, we all piled into my grandparents' station wagon with a "travel bug" on top to hold our luggage and camping equipment. My dad charted our path, and we traveled from one camping site to the next, making interesting stops along the way. Unconcerned with how quickly we could get to a destination, my dad wanted us to have a good time as we traveled.

We were journey travelers, enjoying each step of the journey. My family considered the traveling to be just as important as the actual sites we visited.

On the other hand, my husband and I are destination travelers. We like to plan to visit a particular place, get there as quickly as possible, enjoy our time in that location, and then quickly return home. We don't like to spend a lot of time on the road or in an airplane. We much prefer to enjoy being there!

In our Christian lives, we are often destination travelers instead of journey travelers. We set a goal and want to reach it as quickly as possible. For instance, we want to be able to discern God's will. Perhaps our goal is to know more about the Bible. Once we set a goal, we look for the path of least resistance. How can we reach our goal quickly and easily? Because our minds are focused on accomplishing our goals, we often become frustrated when the process takes more time than we expect. We get angry when obstacles get in the way.

Though Paul had already travelled a long way in his spiritual journey, he recognized he still had a long way to go.

Read Philippians 3:12-16.

Why is it important that we be journey travelers rather than destination travelers in our spiritual lives?

_____

_____

In verse 15 Paul says, "All who are mature should think this way." To what kind of thinking is he referring?

_____

Based on this passage, what is an indicator of spiritual maturity?

_____

Let's look at another important part of the Resource Tool—*Bible commentaries*. These are reference books written by biblical scholars who take portions of the Bible and give detailed notes about the text. (Look on page 68 for an example. There I used a Bible commentary to further clarify what Paul meant in describing his goal.)

Some commentaries are so detailed that they only cover a few chapters of a particular book while others are more broad, covering an entire section of the Bible. You may even find commentaries that discuss the original languages that the Bible was written in, helping you better understand what God was trying to communicate through the authors. On the other hand, some commentaries focus more on the practical applications of Scripture so you can easily understand what God wants to teach you through His Word.

A wide variety of commentaries is available. To find one that will suit your needs, check the appendix on page 112 for recommendations. If you would like to use an online source, go to *www.crosswalk.com*. Click on "Bible Study Tools," and then enter the word or topic you want to find.

Many sites have online commentaries and will let you try several different resources. Choose the one that works for you. You can also visit a Christian book store or ask a trusted pastor or Bible teacher to recommend a commentary for the Bible book you are studying.

When we consult commentaries, we can learn from the research of others. It's as if we are sitting in the classrooms of the great scholars, being taught by those who have dedicated their lives to studying Scripture.

However, always remember that commentaries are written by humans. Unlike Scripture, resource materials may contain errors and speculation. So use your other Bible study tools before consulting commentaries. Always go back to Scripture itself to evaluate what the commentary's author says. If we rely on the Holy Spirit to help us understand the truth of Scripture, then we can more accurately use these other resources.

Read Philippians 3:16.

Consult a commentary to better understand what Paul referred to in Philippians 3:16. What did you learn about this verse? *(Resource Tool)*

_____

_____

_____

What is God wanting to teach you today? *(Application Tool)*

_____

How can you apply this passage to your life? *(Application Tool)*

_____

Write a verse from Philippians 3:12-16 that you can memorize. *(Application Tool)* **Refer to it frequently this week.**

_____

_____

You've worked hard today. Know that God will bless your efforts to learn more about His Word and His character.

Day 4 Changing Our Perspective

One word sums up the key to experiencing joy in every aspect of our lives: perspective. Paul never says that joy will come when we change our circumstances. Instead, he teaches that joy comes when we change our perspective on our circumstances.

This can be a very convicting passage of Scripture, so use your Prayer Tool before you get started. Spend some time praying, and ask God to help you understand what this passage is about; be open to whatever He wants to teach you; and look honestly at any area where you need a change in perspective.

Read Philippians 3:17—4:1.

Paul describes an important contrast in these verses. *(Organization Tool)* **Fill in the following chart with the qualities listed in verses 18-21.**

Enemies of the Cross	Followers of Christ
Their end is _____	Citizenship is in _____
Their god is _____	Eagerly wait for a _____
Glory is in their _____	Our lowly bodies will be _____
Focus is on _____	Christ will _____ everything to Himself

Paul paints a stark contrast between those who follow Christ and those who are enemies of Christ. Jesus did the same thing when He made it clear that we must take a stand when it comes to our relationship with Him: "Anyone who is not with Me is against Me, and anyone who does not gather with Me scatters" (Matt. 12:30).

We cannot "kind of" be for Christ. We must either stand with Him or stand against Him. We will center our perspective either on Christ or on the things of this world. According to Paul, those who are enemies of Christ are focused on the things of this earth. Those who are followers of Christ are focused on things of God. The difference is perspective.

What earthly things distract you from God's purposes for your life?

_____

What process does Paul describe in Philippians 3:20-21?

_____

_____

Name specific ways God has transformed your life.

_____

_____

Thank God for faithfully transforming you. Ask Him to change your perspective so you can appreciate the process rather than focusing on the end result. Thank Him that we know our final destination is in heaven with Him.

Day 5 Handling Conflict

Sometimes when I think about the early churches in the Bible, I imagine they were perfect. After all, if Paul or Peter had written letters to me, I think I would listen to the advice. And if I were being led by one of the apostles who had literally walked with Jesus, surely I would follow his instruction perfectly! But I realize that I wouldn't always follow his wisdom and guidance. We are all human, and we all know failure.

However, I find it encouraging to note that the early church struggled with many of the same issues we struggle with today. Clearly, the early Christians weren't perfect either.

Reread Philippians 1:3-11. You will have a better understanding of these verses now.

Doesn't this passage paint a beautiful picture of a group of believers who are committed to serving Christ faithfully? Paul felt a deep love for them because of all that God had done through them and because of their partnership in the gospel.

Now read today's new verses, Philippians 4:2-3.

Use the Creative Tool with these verses. List each character mentioned. Describe what might have been going on as well as the emotions he or she might have been feeling.

Character	Action	Emotion
_____	_____	_____
_____	_____	_____
	_____	_____
	_____	_____

Euodia and Syntyche had faithfully served with Paul. He knew and loved them both, yet they were not getting along. We don't know exactly what had gone wrong, but we know that the conflict was causing division. Perhaps they were co-hosting a dinner and got in an argument over what should be served. Maybe one had a great ministry idea, but the other didn't like it. One may have been late for a meeting and the other made a sarcastic remark about her tardiness.

You don't have to be around people long to see that conflict is inevitable. However, the conflict itself is not as important as how we handle it.

Use the Scripture Tool to get a more comprehensive look at God's perspective on conflict. Read the following verses to see what the Bible has to say about how to handle conflict. Briefly summarize what each says about this real-life issue.

Psalm 4:4 _____

_____

Proverbs 15:1 _____

_____

Proverbs 17:14 _____

_____

Proverbs 29:11 _____

_____

Matthew 5:23-24 _____

_____

Matthew 18:15-17 _____

_____

1 Corinthians 1:10-18 _____

_____

1 Corinthians 3:1-9 _____

_____

1 Corinthians 13:4-5 _____

_____

Ephesians 4:25-26 _____

_____

Philippians 2:3 _____

_____

1 Thessalonians 5:12-15 _____

_____

James 1:19 _____

_____

What do these verses say about how our perspective can help us avoid unnecessary conflict?

_____

_____

What do these verses tell us about anger?

_____

_____

My husband and I enjoy going to a local video arcade. Our favorite game is _Jurassic Park_. The video game simulates a ride in a Jeep, and players must fight off an onslaught of dinosaurs. In one level, a dinosaur hides in the deep waters of a cove. He raises his head and then disappears back under the water. The eerie silence lures players into complacency. Then, suddenly, the dinosaur shoots out of the water to resume his attack.

Our approach to conflict is often like my complacent approach to that game. As Christians, we sometimes ignore or avoid conflict with the hope that it will just disappear. Unfortunately, that rarely happens. Instead, like the dinosaur in our game, conflict hides just below the surface before it raises its ugly head.

Conflict can be very destructive, causing division, bitterness, and unforgiveness. However, it can also be a powerful tool that leads to greater intimacy with God. As we humbly and lovingly deal with our problems, relying on God's wisdom and guidance to face them, we gain a better understanding of each other. In fact, weathering conflict can even help us to grow closer to God and one another.

Even if we have to agree to disagree, we can choose to live in harmony as we work together to accomplish God's purposes. When we choose to forgive one another, we give the same kind of unconditional love that Christ gave to us.

We can experience joy in the midst of conflict, but we must have God's perspective on the situation. We must choose to reflect His character and live out His commands in the midst of the disagreement. We must remember that:

"All things work together for the good of those who love God: those who are called according to His purpose" (Rom. 8:28).

Basing your response on Romans 8:28, describe how you can improve your reactions to conflict.

_____

_____

_____

_____

_____

_____

Paul is about to bring closure to this amazing book of the Bible. The last chapter contains more than final instructions; much of the meat of this book is still to come. You'll be glad you stayed with it till the end.

How's It Going?

Have you noticed I've not sent you to "Tianne's Answers" recently? That's because you're able to find the answers on your own!

I can't believe that we are at the end of week 4 and nearing the end of our study together. I hope that the Bible study tools you are using will continue to help you as you spend time in God's Word!

Staying on Course with God

VIEWER GUIDE

STAY ON COURSE BY STAYING CLOSE TO THE MASTER WHO GUIDES US

The Lord is near. Will He find us staying the course or tugging at the leash?

"Squirrels" That Pull Us Off Course

1. The Squirrel of _____

   We often start worrying before we even realize what we're

   doing. When tempted to chase the squirrel of worry,

   we need to _____ _____ _____

2. The Squirrel of _____

   Focusing on the negative gets us off course from what God

   wants in our lives. Focusing on the _____

   will help get us back on track.

3. The Squirrel of _____

   Remember that _____ can do so much more than

   we can imagine or do for ourselves.

> *"Rejoice in the Lord always ... The Lord is near."*
> *Philippians 4:4-5*

In-Touch or Out-of-Control?

Emotions add much color and beauty to life! But we don't want our emotions to be so out-of-control that we irrationally travel through life, being blown around by our feelings.

Instead of being governed by our emotions, we need to stay in touch with the truth. Regardless of what feelings enter our lives, we should filter each through the truth of Scripture so we can have God's perspective on our circumstances.

Worry is one of the emotions that can quickly control us. Our battle with worry is fought on the front lines of our minds. This week, we will explore how to win the battle over worry, learning how to rely on others when we become battle-weary.

I hope you are becoming more comfortable with the Bible study tools as we enter our last week of this study. As you continue to use them, you will grow more confident in approaching any passage of Scripture. You will examine passages to gather details and background information. You will filter the insight you gain through prayer and research, gleaning principles that you can apply to your life. And most importantly—you will experience the life-changing power of God's Word.

Remember, changing your circumstances is not the key to experiencing thirst-quenching joy in every area of your life. Instead, the key to discovering joy is changing your perspective on your circumstances. As you see your life through God's eyes, you will develop His perspective and find the satisfaction that comes from walking closely with Him.

The One who created you and loves you is the One who can best show you how to experience total satisfaction—no matter where you are on your journey.

Day 1 Giving Thanks
in Everything

Throughout this study we have talked about perspective. When we align our perspective with God's and trust that He is working in all of our circumstances, we become positioned to experience joy. Experiencing joy in all circumstances must start in our minds. Paul shows us some helpful strategies to help us change our perspective.

Briefly note a description of each of the Bible-study tools.

1. Question Tool _____

2. Application Tool _____

3. Creative Tool _____

4. Scripture Tool _____

5. Relationship Tool _____

6. Organization Tool _____

7. Prayer Tool _____

8. Resource Tool _____

Read Philippians 4:4-7, and then choose three of the tools to help you draw out the details of the passage.

1. _____

_____

2. _____

_____

3. _____

_____

Which tools did you find most helpful? After I read Philippians 4:4-7, I used the **Question Tool** to pull out some of the details:

When are we to rejoice? Always!

Who should be able to see our graciousness? Everyone!

Why does it say "The Lord is near"? This may be a reminder that He is always present and aware of our actions, or it may be a reference to the time Christ will return—so we shouldn't waste any time!

When is it OK to worry? Never!

When should we pray? Always!

Then I noted the words "but" and "and" in the verses, so I used the **Relationship Tool** to note contrasts and comparisons:

Don't worry *but* let your requests be made known to God

Prayer *and* petition *with* thanksgiving

Cause and effect: prayer *that* leads to peace

Finally, I used the **Organization Tool** to write out the sequence I noted in this passage:

Don't worry—

    Pray with thanksgiving—

        Peace beyond understanding—

            Guard heart and mind

In the fourth chapter of Philippians, Paul began to wrap up his letter. In doing so, he summarized the keys to having joy in all things. He commands us to rejoice but acknowledges that one of the barriers to rejoicing is worry.

According to Paul, what helps us combat worries that steal our joy?

_____

What are the results of following his instructions?

_____

Paul addressed the same topic in 1 Thessalonians 5:16-18. *(Scripture Tool)* According to these verses, what will help us to "rejoice always!"?

_____

Why is prayer an important tool in combating our worries?

_____

_____

Paul's command to give thanks in all circumstances seems like an impossible task until we realize that he commands us to give thanks _in_ all circumstances—not _for_ all circumstances.

Sometimes everything in life seems to be going well. Our careers are on track. Our relationships are healthy. The sun is shining, and it seems that God's blessings are overflowing. We can easily thank God when life is pleasant, just as we can easily smile when we are pleased. But during the tough times—those days when hardship and sadness overwhelm us—we might find it difficult to give thanks for our circumstances.

God reminds us again that we will often find ourselves in circumstances we cannot change. When we find ourselves in the middle of those difficult circumstances, the only thing we can change is our perspective. Instead of focusing on what is not going our way, we can focus on the things that are going our way. We can choose to thank God for the good things in our lives—the things that we often take for granted.

Describe a difficult situation that you have recently had to face.

_____

_____

_____

_____

_____

Name four things for which you can thank God about that situation.

_____   _____

_____   _____

When we are in the midst of difficult times, we can easily give in to human nature by wishing things were different. But instead of wishing away life's negatives, we should get in the habit of regularly thanking God for the good things in our lives. As we develop that habit, we will find that we can experience the joy that comes from recognizing the blessings in life. As we focus on the positive, we will be able to energize and encourage those around us.

Recently, a friend was killed in a car accident. The next morning, his wife was overwhelmed with the grief of losing her husband. In a moment her life had completely changed, and she could do nothing to go back to the way it was before. At that point, she was not able to thank God for taking her husband, but she did thank God for promising never to leave or forsake her (Heb. 13:5). She relied on His promise to comfort all who mourn (Isa. 61:1-3).

When we choose to rejoice, we are not choosing to deny the painful things in our lives. Instead, we are choosing to trust God in the midst of the pain.

Prayer is key to this process. When we pray, we exercise our faith.

Through prayer we say to God:

"I can't handle this, but I know You can."

"I can't understand this, but I know You have the answers."

"I can't face tomorrow alone, but I know You will be there."

When I am really thirsty, the one thing I want is an ice-cold drink that will refresh and satisfy me. The last thing I want is something salty because I know that the saltiness will only make my thirst greater.

Worry is like drinking saltwater when I long to have my thirst satisfied. If I take my worries to God, thanking Him for what He has done and trusting in what He will do in the future, I will experience the joy that comes from letting Him carry my heavy load. I will finally experience satisfaction.

What are some of the things you worry about?

_____   _____

_____   _____

Take a few minutes to ask God to handle the worry, pain, and difficulty in your life. Thank Him for being big enough to handle it all.

Day 2 Fighting with Truth

Scripture teaches that we can intentionally choose to fill our minds with good and positive thoughts. If we go to Him in prayer, God will fill our minds with His truth. Let's take a close look at what Paul says about thoughts.

Read Philippians 4:8-9, and circle the eight words in verse 8 that describe what we are to think about. *(Organization Tool)*

Philippians 4:8-9

[8] Finally brothers, whatever is true, whatever is honorable, whatever is just, whatever is pure, whatever is lovely, whatever is commendable—if there is any moral excellence and if there is any praise—dwell on these things. [9] Do what you have learned and received and heard and seen in me, and the God of peace will be with you.

Over the next few hours, pay close attention to the things you think about when your mind wanders and you do not have to focus on anything in particular. Take notice of what came to mind, and then list those things below.

_____

_____

_____

_____

Recently, I caught myself thinking negatively. Imagining a worst-case scenario, I practiced for an anticipated conflict. Then I began thinking about another challenge and started worrying about all the things that could go wrong—even though I knew everything would turn out all right.

Our minds are often like magnets, gravitating toward life's negatives. When we become consumed with negative thoughts, we lose our joy. That's why Paul commands us to deliberately think on things that are positive and true.

Read 2 Corinthians 10:3-5. *(Scripture Tool)* Then use the Question Tool to find out the following information.

What kind of battle are we fighting?

_____

What kind of weapons are we using?

_____

Our minds are spiritual battlefields where Satan begins his attack, trying to rob us of all joy and victory in our lives. If he can distract us with his lies, then we will enter the battle on our own strength instead of relying on God's power and guidance. If the devil can distract us from what is true and right, then he can keep us from the joy God wants to give us.

Too often, we try to fight spiritual battles with earthly weapons such as the following excuses:

"I just need to try harder."

"If I had more money, I wouldn't worry so much."

"If I lost some weight, I wouldn't be so lonely."

"If I were talented like she is, I would be happier."

We think we can experience joy by changing our earthly circumstances, so we fight by focusing on earthly things such as personal effort, money, appearance, and abilities. Instead of centering on ourselves or earthly things, we need to fight with spiritual weapons. We must focus on what is true and right. Then we will be equipped to fight against our enemy.

Read Ephesians 6:10-20 to learn more about our spiritual weapons. Based on this passage, label the pieces of our spiritual armor.

Enjoy

Let's take a quick look at this spiritual armor. As we try to find out more about being outfitted for spiritual battle, we'll use our Scripture Tool quite a bit, and appropriately so. I'll designate the other tools I will use in case you are uncertain which ones are being used.

The first piece of the armor is listed in verse 14: the belt of truth. This piece holds the rest of our armor together. If we do not know, believe, and apply the truth to our lives, we will be defenseless.

Read John 8:44. *(Scripture Tool)*

How **is Satan described in this verse?** *(Question Tool)*

_____

_____

What are some of the lies that you have believed about ...

yourself? _____

God? _____

how God works in your life? _____

What habits have you built into your life to make sure you know and apply the truth of God's Word? *(Application Tool)*

_____

_____

Notice that Paul doesn't say the belt of truth will jump on your body! In the Ephesians passage he tells us we are to "put on" each piece of the armor (6:11,14-17). We put on the belt of truth by regularly learning the truth—found in the Bible—and then putting it to work in our lives. We need to read the Bible and apply what we learn. We need to put it into action.

As I apply the truth to my life, I build on the firm foundation of Christ. Being anchored to Him, I won't be tossed around by my feelings, the opinions of others, or life's circumstances. Instead, I will be able to stand strong against Satan's onslaught, and I will experience joy because my life is built on Christ.

Paul then describes the breastplate of righteousness. This piece of armor protects us from neck to waist on the front and back.

Read carefully 2 Corinthians 5:21. *(Scripture Tool)*
When Jesus died for you on the cross, a great exchange took place. The sin that you carry in your life was put on Jesus, and His perfection was given to you. So now, when God looks at you, He doesn't see someone who has repeatedly failed to live up to His standards. Instead, He sees His perfect Son. This does not mean that you will never sin again. Rather, it means that one day when you stand before God, He will not condemn you because of your sin. He will see you as if you are perfect like His Son. When you choose to accept Jesus as your Savior, you are agreeing to this exchange—and God will never look at you the same way again.

Read 1 John 1:9. *(Scripture Tool)*

This Scripture is key when we are fighting spiritual battles. Satan loves to tell us that the exchange never took place, that we are still marked by our sin, and that we have no choice but to give in to temptation. Listening to these lies will rob us of joy because we will either wilt under our shame or we will wear ourselves out trying to be good enough for God. We need to remember the truth that God has already told us: He loves us, and we can stand against anything—even Satan—if we depend on Him.
    Let's look at the next piece of the armor: the sandals of the gospel.

What does *gospel* mean? (Use your Resource Tool to look up its definition, or find other Scriptures that mention the word *gospel*.)

Read 1 Corinthians 15:1-8. *(Scripture Tool)*

The gospel is the good news that Jesus died in our place and then rose again on the third day. We can stand firm because we are standing on this truth. However, the gospel also shows us the importance of sharing our faith.

Read Romans 10:13-15. *(Scripture Tool)*
We need to be prepared to tell others about this good news that we have experienced in our own lives. When I am actively sharing what Jesus has done in my life, I experience joy as I tell my story and as I see God reach out to those around me. Telling the world about Jesus is the greatest way to fight against what Satan wants to do in our world!

The shield of faith is another essential piece of our spiritual armor. Trusting in God's promises and power will protect us from the flaming arrows of doubt that can destroy our lives.

In what areas of life do you have trouble trusting God to handle everything? *(Application Tool)*

_____

_____

_____

When we faithfully trust God, look forward to the future with joy. We can withstand the fires of doubt that Satan tries to start.

The helmet of salvation is the part of the armor that protects our head. The helmet is a reminder to protect your mind with the truth about who God is and what He has done for you.

When I was a physical therapy student, I had the opportunity to watch several autopsies. I will never forget the drug dealer who was brought down to the morgue. At the time of his murder, he was armed and was wearing a bulletproof vest. But all that protection didn't matter because someone shot him in the head. How ironic! He thought he was ready for battle, but he didn't protect an organ that is essential to life—his brain.

We must protect our minds. If we don't, then we will be vulnerable to Satan's subtle strategies. We must fill our minds with the truth of God and protect ourselves from the lies of the evil one.

Let's take a look at the last piece of the armor: the sword of the Spirit.

What is the "sword of the Spirit" (Eph. 6:17)? *(Question Tool)*

_____

How does the Word of God, the Bible, equip us to fight against the evil one? *(Question Tool)*

_____

_____

_____

Which piece of armor is used as an offensive rather than
a defensive weapon?

_____

What does Paul command us to do in Ephesians 6:18?

_____

Isn't it interesting that our primary offensive weapon against our enemy
is the sword of the Spirit—God's Word? What is Paul saying? He is telling
us that our greatest weapon against the evil one is the Bible. If we were to
summarize what the armor of God is, we could say that it is knowing,
believing, and living out God's truth in every part of our lives.

When we fill our minds with the truth and choose to focus on positive
things, we are well on our way to experiencing joy and victory. However,
staying focused on the truth of God's Word requires discipline. We must:
1. stop ourselves when we begin to think negatively.
2. ask God to fill our minds with His truth.
3. intentionally think about things that are positive and true.
Try putting these things into practice, and note how they change your
outlook. Watch as God reshapes your perspective on your circumstances
and brings joy into your life.

Day 3 Giving of Ourselves

Today we will learn the secret of being content in all situations. Remember,
contentment does not necessarily mean that we will not have struggles.
Let's take a look at Paul's explanation of contentment.

Read Philippians 4:10-13.

List the circumstances Paul describes in these verses. (When you
do, you are using the Organization Tool.)

_____

_____

_____

What are some of the negative circumstances in Paul's life that you have learned about over the past several weeks? *(Question Tool)*

_____

_____

_____

How do you think Paul felt as he wrote Philippians 4:10-13? *(Creative Tool)*

_____

_____

_____

Describe a time when you felt content. *(Application Tool)*

_____

Describe the feeling of contentment. *(Application Tool)*

_____

Did your description of contentment focus on your circumstances or on your perspective on those circumstances?

❏ circumstances   ❏ perspective

What secret to contentment did Paul discover?

_____

When most of us think about being content, we picture a time in our lives when everything has fallen into place. We imagine a time without financial struggles, relationship problems, or work worries. We may picture ourselves on an idealistic day filled with sunshine, surrounded by people we love. (And of course we are all getting along perfectly!)

In verse 12, Paul offered a very different view of contentment. He described contentment as being independent of our circumstances. He emphasized that joy comes from our perspective, not our surroundings.

Paul's contentment and joy came from knowing that he could handle anything. This confidence was not based on his own abilities to deal with his life but on knowing that God would give him the strength he needed to deal with all circumstances.

Describe a time in your life when you were discontent.

_____

_____

_____

What were the circumstances behind your discontentment?

_____

_____

What was your perspective on your circumstances?

_____

What was your attitude toward your circumstances?

_____

Read Philippians 4:4-13.

In the future, how can you adjust your perspective so that you experience joy in negative circumstances?

_____

Pray and ask God to help you adjust your perspective. Ask Him to help you trust in Him in the midst of challenging circumstances.

Read Philippians 4:14-20.

What is the first word in this passage? _(Question Tool)_

_____

The word *still* indicates a contrast. What things are being contrasted? *(Relationship Tool, Scripture Tool)*

_____

_____

In Philippians 4:14-20 Paul said he was content even in need because he knew that God would help him handle anything. As I studied this passage, I noticed that verse 14 started with the word "still." Paul says: "Still, you did well by sharing with me in my hardship."

Having never noticed that sentence before, I was surprised when it seemed to jump off the page at me. Paul described a very important balance. Even though we may be content in the midst of our difficulties; though we may fully trust that God is going to provide all we need; it is still comforting when others share in our troubles.

Being content and joyful in the midst of pain does not mean we no longer need the comfort and love of others. In fact in our time of need, God often provides for us through others.

A few days ago, I mentioned a friend who grieved over the sudden death of her husband. It has been remarkable to see how God has given her peace, comfort, and strength. Equally inspiring is how God provided people to stand beside her and walk with her through that difficult time. Their comfort and help have been invaluable evidence of God's love. They have brought her much joy in the face of intense grief.

It shouldn't surprise us that in the final chapter of Philippians Paul again referred to the wonderful relationship he had with the people of Philippi. He started his beautiful letter by describing the joy they had brought him. He ended it by again describing the joy they continued to bring as they shared in His work.

Whom has God brought into your life to help you through difficulties?

_____

Stop for a moment and thank God for these people.

Read Philippians 4:18-19.

How **did Paul describe their gifts?** *(Question Tool)*

_____

Read Romans 12:1-2. *(Scripture Tool)*

Paul used very similar language in these two passages. As he received gifts, he didn't just see them as gifts to him—he saw them as gifts to God. As the Philippians gave to Paul, they also worshiped God.

List ways that you have given to others in the past week.

_____

We can give to others in many creative ways. For instance:
- A single mom is battling cancer, and a friend offers to drive her to and from her chemotherapy treatments each week.
- A young couple has their first child, and several friends provide meals for several weeks so the new family can get settled.
- Families with special-needs children are unable to attend church because no one can provide adequate childcare. A group of volunteers begins a ministry to care for these children while their parents attend worship services each week.
- A young man is unable to pay medical bills, so friends in his Bible study group take up a collection to help with his expenses.

When we give to others—financially, emotionally, spiritually, or physically—we give to God and worship Him. Isn't that wonderful? We can actually be a part of what God wants to do in someone else's life by giving generously of our time, money, and resources.

I can be generous—even in tight financial times—because God has promised to meet all my needs. I can be generous—even with a busy schedule—because God has promised to give me the strength to do everything He asks of me.

What is one way you can give to someone this week?

_____

A beautiful joy comes when we experience the generosity of others and when we choose to give to the people in our lives.

Day 4 Committing
Myself to God

When I study a book of the Bible that was originally written as a letter,
I sometimes run quickly through the opening and closing greetings.
But if we do that here we miss out on some very important details.

Read Philippians 4:21-23.

To whom did Paul send greetings in verse 21?

_____

**What does it mean to be a "saint"? (Use the Resource Tool. Look
in a Bible dictionary to find the definition. Or look up "saint" in a
word concordance to find other Bible verses that use this word.)**

_____

_____

_____

Throughout Scripture, we see the word *saint* used to describe anyone
who is a Christ-follower. You don't have to live an extraordinary life or
receive extraordinary recognition to be called a saint. The Bible says that
you are extraordinary simply because you belong to Christ. You don't
have to try and earn the title; you are given the title because you are a
loved child of God. Don't ever forget that!

From whom does Paul send greetings in verse 22? *(Question Tool)*

_____

Caesar was the ruler of the Roman empire. Apparently some members
of his household had become Christ-followers.

Read Philippians 1:12-13. *(Scripture Tool)*

In chapter 1, Paul made it clear that he considered his imprisonment to be
a new opportunity to fulfill his purpose—to tell others about Jesus Christ.

In chapter 4, Paul indicated that this purpose had been accomplished in the household of the most powerful man in Rome.

The two parts of this story serve as wonderful bookends to this book about joy. Once again we see that Paul experienced joy because he saw every circumstance as an opportunity for God to carry out His purpose. What a fitting end to this book!

When I look at Paul, I sometimes think, *Well, of course he experienced joy in his life! Look at all the incredible things that God did through him! If God used me like that, I'd be full of joy too!* But we have learned enough about Paul to know he often found himself in very trying circumstances. The biggest difference between Paul and us is that we often focus on our circumstances rather than on how God wants to work in our circumstances.

Spend time just talking with and listening to God. I have never heard God's audible voice, but many times He has spoken to my heart—bringing thoughts to my mind, reminding me of Scripture that I have read, clearing up confusion about a situation, or comforting my troubled mind with His peace.

Find a quiet place where you can be uninterrupted for at least 10 minutes and talk to God. Remember to ...
- **thank Him for some specific things He is doing in your life.**
- **confess any areas in which you are not trusting Him.**
- **ask Him for help in areas in which you are not experiencing joy.**
- **thank Him that we can count on His promises.**

Read Philippians 3:7-11 and rewrite this passage in your own words as your prayer of commitment to God.

_____

_____

_____

_____

_____

_____

Spend some quiet time listening to God.

Day 5 Living Joyfully

When we look at Paul, we can easily focus on his many accomplishments, the people he touched, and his strong convictions. But we need to also remember that he was a man God transformed. He encountered Jesus and his life was forever changed.

What about you? What has happened to you since you encountered Jesus Christ? Do you see life through His eyes, or are you still looking through your own lenses?

This study of Philippians has been a refreshing reminder of the life God wants for each of us. He doesn't want us to drown under the weight of our struggles, and He wants us to fully enjoy the good things in our lives. However, that can only happen when we decide to get our minds, hearts, and actions in line with Him.

Someone once asked me if I thought joy was a feeling or a choice. Interesting question! When I look through Scripture, I see both. Joy is often contrasted with sorrow and is associated with celebration, so it is definitely an emotion. But when I read Bible verses that talk about joy, the consistent pattern is this: joy comes from God, specifically when I choose to align myself with Him.

If I want to experience ultimate joy and satisfaction as I walk through life, I must choose to get my perspective, my attitude, and my choices in line with God. In its simplest form, joy comes down to obedience.

- When I choose to forgive and humbly love someone who has hurt me, I am choosing obedience to God. I can experience joy because I know I am aligning my life with His will.

- When I choose to congratulate and support someone who got the promotion I wanted, I am choosing obedience to God. I can experience joy because I am aligning my life with His will.

- When I choose to remain sexually pure even though I am lonely and longing for a husband and family, I am choosing obedience to God. I can experience joy because I am aligning my life with His will.

Read Galatians 5:16-26. *(Scripture Tool)*

What is being contrasted in verses 16-18? *(Relationship Tool)*

_____

_____

List the characteristics from verses 19-21 that mark someone who is living by the flesh (sinful nature). *(Organization Tool)*

_____

_____

_____

_____

List the characteristics from verses 22-23 that mark someone who is living by the Spirit. *(Organization Tool)*

_____

_____

Joy is a fruit of the Spirit. Therefore, I cannot produce it; the Holy Spirit must produce it in me. But I must choose to live by the Spirit so that my life is aligned with God and He can begin to work in me.

Take a few minutes to read your notes from this study. List one or two things God has taught you that you want to apply to your life.

Week 1 _____

_____

_____

Week 2 _____

_____

_____

Week 3 _____

_____

_____

Week 4 _____

_____

_____

Week 5 _____

_____

_____

Now, let's make a plan to put these things into practice. Consider the following questions as you look at areas in which you can choose joy.

What circumstance in your life is robbing you of joy?

_____

_____

How can you change your perspective on this circumstance?

_____

_____

What choice(s) do you need to make in this circumstance so you can align yourself with God?

_____

_____

What have you learned from this study that will help you to have joy in this situation?

_____

_____

Texas has some intensely hot summer days. When I am in the middle of one of those days, perspiring and longing for a cool breeze, nothing refreshes me like an ice cold glass of lemonade! But I've noticed that even though that drink is refreshing, it doesn't actually change my circumstances. I still perspire and it is still intensely hot, but it's just that I feel a little better in the midst of it all. Lemonade can go a long way in getting me through the heat!

We sometimes find ourselves in the middle of pretty intense circumstances that leave us longing for a fresh, cool breeze. Often we desire something to get us through the heat, and God's joy does exactly that—it refreshes us. While the joy that comes from the Lord does not necessarily change your current circumstances, it can help you feel better in the midst of them. Isn't it great to know that God cares enough for you to quench your thirst?

What a blessing to spend this time with you! Your commitment to following God faithfully inspires and encourages me.

"I give thanks to my God for every remembrance of you" (Phil. 1:3).

Learning Contentment

VIEWER GUIDE

CONTENTMENT IS INDEPENDENT
OF OUR CIRCUMSTANCES

Contentment Is Not ...

1. _____

2. _____

Contentment Is ...

1. _____ God's plan (4:11)

2. _____ in God's strength (4:13)

God can be glorified when we are aware of our
weakness and His strength.

"I have learned to be content
in whatever circumstances I am ...
I am able to do all things through Him
who strengthens me"—
Philippians 4:11,13.

How to Become a Christian

Jesus taught that life is more than physical existence. He desires a relationship with us that satisfies and refreshes our hearts and minds. He offers us eternal life, forgiveness, hope, peace, and joy—each a wonderful gift that comes with a personal relationship with God.

To live this life "to the full" (see John 10:10), we must first accept God's incredible gift of love: Jesus. John 3:16 says, "God loved the world in this way: He gave His One and Only Son, so that everyone who believes in Him will not perish but have eternal life."

A relationship with God begins by admitting that you are not perfect and continue to fall short of God's standards. Romans 3:23 says, "All have sinned and fall short of the glory of God." The price for these wrong-doings is separation from God. And we deserve to pay the price for our sin. "The wages (or price) of sin (wrong-doing) is death, but the gift of God is eternal life in Christ Jesus our Lord" (Rom. 6:23).

God's love extends to us in our imperfection. "God proves His own love for us in that while we were still sinners Christ died for us" (Rom. 5:8)!

Forgiveness begins when we admit our sins to God. When we do, He is faithful to forgive us and to restore our relationship with Him. "If we confess our sins, He is faithful and righteous to forgive us our sins and to cleanse us from all unrighteousness" (1 John 1:9).

Romans 10:13 confirms that this love gift and relationship with God is not just for a special few but for everyone. "Everyone who calls on the name of the Lord will be saved."

If you would like to receive God's gift of salvation, pray this prayer:

Dear God, I know that I am imperfect and separated from You. Please forgive me of my sin and adopt me as Your child. Thank you for this gift of life through the sacrifice of your Son. I will live my life for You. Amen.

If you sincerely prayed this prayer, you are now a child of God! In your Bible, read 1 John 5:11-12. This verse assures you that if you have accepted God's Son, Jesus Christ, as your Savior and Lord, you have eternal life.

Share your experience with your *Enjoy* facilitator, someone in your group, your pastor, or a trusted Christian friend.

Welcome to God's family! And enjoy your relationship with Him. He loves you so much!

Tianne's Answers

You won't find the answers to every activity on these pages. Many of the answers will become clear as you read Scripture. But often when you are learning to use a tool for the first time, I'll share my responses to help you check your progress. Remember, in many cases, there are no right or wrong answers. And you should always do the activities before looking to these pages for help.

Each week when you meet with your small group, your facilitator and the other participants can share their insights.

Week One

Viewer Guide

choices; environment; competition; life, death; relationships; glorify Him

Day 1

Read John 14:23-27.

Circle what verses 25-26 promise us about the Holy Spirit.

²³Jesus answered, "If anyone loves Me, he will keep My word. My Father will love him, and We will come to him and make Our home with him. ²⁴The one who doesn't love Me will not keep My words. The word that you hear is not Mine but is from the Father who sent Me. ²⁵"I have spoken these things to you while I remain with you. ²⁶But the Counselor, the Holy Spirit—whom the Father will send in My name—will teach you all things and remind you of everything I have told you. ²⁷"Peace I leave with you. My peace I give to you. I do not give to you as the world gives. Your heart must not be troubled or fearful."

What should be the result of our embracing this promise? Peace

Who was writing this letter (v. 1)? Paul
Who was it written to (v. 1)? Philippian church
Where was this letter being sent (v. 1)? Philippi
How did the letter writer feel about these people (vv. 3-4)? Joyful
Why did Paul feel this way about them (vv. 5-8)? Their partnership in the gospel
What was he sure of (v. 6)? God will complete His work in them

What did Paul pray for (v. 9)?   Both love and discernment will grow
Why did he pray this prayer (vv. 10-11)?   For them to be pure and
blameless, filled with righteousness

Day 2

Who is this passage about?   Paul
What has happened to Paul?   imprisonment
What are the results of Paul's imprisonment?   Gospel advanced
Why were others encouraged to preach more courageously?
Gained confidence in Paul's imprisonment

Day 3

Read Philippians 1:15-18 and answer the following questions.

What are the two types of people described in this passage (v. 15)?
Those preaching out of love and those preaching out of envy
Those preaching out of good will were motivated by _love_ (v. 16).
What was Paul appointed to defend (v. 16)?   The gospel
Those preaching out of envy and strife, those who preached
out of _good_ _will_ (v. 17).
Those preaching out of envy and strife were motivated out of
rivalry (v. 17).
How did those not motivated by love hope to impact Paul (v. 17)?
Cause him trouble in prison
In the midst of all that was happening in this competition, *what*
was most important to Paul (v. 18)?   That Christ be proclaimed
Because of this focus, *how* did Paul respond to Christ's message
being proclaimed (v. 18)?   He rejoiced

Day 4

Questions from Philippians 1:19-26:
You likely gave different questions and answers, but here are some facts
I discovered. Note that this passage lends itself to certain question-starters
(what, why) more than others (where, how).

Who?
To whom is Paul writing this passage?   The Philippians
Who is receiving the message?   The Philippians—close friends
who were committed to God
What?
What is going to bring about Paul's "deliverance"?   The prayers
of his friends and the help of the Holy Spirit

What is Paul choosing between?   Living for Christ or dying so he can
    be with Christ

What does he consider to be the better option?   Dying and being
    with Christ

What will keep Paul from being ashamed?   Being able to show
    courage while living

What is Paul's goal for the Philippians?   That they will both continue
    to grow in faith and also experience joy in their faith

When?

When did Paul feel he would be most fruitful?   In his death

Why?

Why does Paul feel torn?   He wants to be with Christ, but he knows
    that it is best to stay and help his friends, the Philippians.

Why does Paul say "living is Christ and dying is gain"?   He wins
    either way! While he is alive, he will be living for Christ. When
    he dies, it will be even better because he will get to see Christ.

Where?

Where was it best for Paul to remain?   This world, to minister

How?

How did Paul view his ministry?   As necessary for the Philippians

What do followers of Christ gain when they die?

    John 14:2   Place prepared for them in heaven

    2 Corinthians 4:17   Incomparable glory

    Philippians 3:20-21   Heavenly citizenship; transformed bodies

    Revelation 7:16-17   No hunger or thirst

    Revelation 21:1-4   New heaven and new earth; God's dwelling
        with them; His comfort; no more death

    Revelation 22:1-5   Experiencing the city of God with the Lamb
        of God; service to God; eternal reign

Week Two

Viewer Guide

not equal; loved; why, obey; Attitudes; Actions

Day 2

What is compared in verse 5?   Attitudes—mine and Christ's

What does the contrast in verses 6-7 tell us about Christ's nature?
Verse 6-existing as God, Christ became man

> **What** qualities are used to describe Christ in verse 7?   Emptied
> Himself, assumed form of a slave, took on human likeness
> **What** were the results of Jesus' humbling Himself?   Obedience
> and death

Day 3

Here are some details I found using these tools to address Philippians 2:12-13:

Question Tool (Details Matter)

Why does Paul refer to the Philippians as "dear friends"?   He is
reaffirming his commitment to their friendship and partnership.
Why were they still obedient?   They were so committed to Christ that
they continued to be obedient without Paul's presence.

Application Tool (What's the Bottom Line?)

Bottom line: There is a point when I have to stop doing the right thing
because someone is watching. I must do the right thing in response
to the God I serve. When I humble myself before Him and give Him
control, then He can work out His will and purpose for my life. This
passage makes me ask the question, "Does God have control of me?"

Creative Tool (Imagine the Emotions)

The Philippians may have felt fear that they would suddenly lose Paul's
guidance. But they probably also felt a sense of relief at Paul's confidence
in their ability to trust in the Lord without Paul's continued support.

Scripture Tool (Other Verses Help)

Look for verses about:
Words: Salvation, Fear, Fear and trembling
Topics: Grace (see Eph. 2:8-10; Titus 2-3), Faith (see Romans),
Righteousness

Relationship Tool (The Three C's)

"But"	Contrast, presence vs. absence
"And"	Comparison, "fear" and "trembling"
"And"	God works in you "to will" and "to act"
"Therefore"	Cause-and-effect; In verses 1-11, Paul discusses the importance of unity and humility. "Therefore" we should respond by continuing to work out our salvation "with fear and trembling."

If you were able to pull out some of these details, then you are on the right track!

Week Three

Viewer Guide

heritage, come from; appearance, look; achievements, have done; possessions, have; spirituality, believe

Day 2

When I used the Relationship Tool, I noticed a contrast between the people described in verses 2 and 3, so I used the Organization Tool to make a list of their differences.

Verse 2	Verse 3
Dogs	The circumcision
Evil ones	Worship by the Spirit of God
Mutilators of the flesh	Glory in Christ, put no confidence in the flesh

Noticing that both lists refer to "the flesh," I used a topical concordance to find other verses that also mention "the flesh," otherwise referred to as our sinful nature. Here's what I found:

Romans 7:18-25	The sinful nature in me has no good in it
Romans 8:8-13	Living by the sinful nature leads to death
Galatians 5:17	Our sinful nature and the Spirit are in conflict
Galatians 6:8	What you sow, you will reap
1 John 2:16	The flesh wants what the world offers, not what the Father wants

These tools helped me realize that Paul was using a play on words. In Philippians 3:2, he refers to a literal mutilation of the flesh—physical circumcision. In verse 3, he refers to the spiritual circumcision that we experience when we give our lives to Christ and are marked by the Holy Spirit. We do not trust in our own abilities or efforts; we rely on Christ for all things.

Day 3

If you had looked up *flesh* in a Bible dictionary, you might find this information: The term *flesh* can be a neutral term referring to created humans and animals who are limited and weak, or it can refer to humans controlled by sin and its passions.

Week Four

Viewer Guide

Basking, glory; Bowing, weight; Biding time; Being distracted

Day 1

questions; details; Summarize; learn; apply; memorize; creatively; emotions; verses; contrasts; comparisons; cause; effect; details; lists; Pray; resources

Week Five

Viewer Guide

Worry, pray it through; Negativity, positive; Complacency, God

Week Six

Viewer Guide

Quitting; Settling; Accepting; Trusting

Resources for Further Study

Atlas

Holman Bible Atlas
Hardcover: 1558197095

Bibles

Harmony of the Gospels
Hardcover: 0805494235

Holman CSB
Hardcover: 158640068-1

The Message (paraphrase)
Hardcover: 1576832899

Bible Dictionary

Holman Bible Dictionary
Hardcover: 1558190538

Electronic Media

Holman CSB Bible Navigator–CD
1586400789

Crosswalk
bible.crosswalk.com
bible.crosswalk.com/ParallelBible

LifeWay's Online Bible Library
lifeway.com

www.lifeway.com/newsletters
eSolutions for Women's Ministry
women's ministry link on the Web
Inspired Living
Ministers' Wives Update
Women's e-Study Wire
Women's Resources and Events Update

How to Have a Daily Quiet Time

1. Make a personal quiet time your top priority. Select a time to spend with God that fits your schedule. Usually, morning is preferable, but you may want or need to choose another time.

2. Prepare the night before.

- If your quiet time is in the morning, set an alarm. If you have difficulty waking up, bathe, dress, and eat before your quiet time.

- Select a place where you can be alone. Gather your Bible, notebook, and a pen, putting them in the place you select.

3. Develop a balanced plan of Bible reading and prayer.

- Pray for guidance during your quiet time.

- Follow a systematic plan to read your Bible. Use a devotional guide if desired.

- Make notes of what God says to you through His Word.

- Pray in response to the Scriptures you read. Using the acronym ACTS—adoration, confession, thanksgiving, supplication—helps you remember the components of prayer.

4. Be persistent until you are consistent.

- Strive for consistency rather than length (spend a few minutes of quiet time every day rather than having a long devotional every two days).

- Expect and plan for interruptions. Satan tries to prevent you from spending time with God. He fears the prayers of even the weakest Christians. Plan around interruptions rather than being frustrated by them.

5. Focus on meeting with God. God created you with a capacity for fellowship with Him, and He saved you to bring about that fellowship.[1]

[1]Adapted from Avery T. Willis, Jr., *MasterLife 1: The Disciple's Cross* (Nashville: LifeWay, 1996) 19-20.

Leader Guide

Introduction

Welcome! Thank you for your willingness to serve as a a leader for *Enjoy: A Thirst-Quenching Look at Philippians*. This guide will help you facilitate six sessions which include large-group video teaching and small-group discussion time. Each weekly lesson plan contains a creative learning activity and a guide for reviewing the weekly assigments through the use of discussion questions.

Feel free to adapt these materials to fit the needs of your group.

Environment

Since we come from different backgrounds and experiences, sensitivity toward one another is important. Don't assume that everyone in your group is just like you. (And don't be concerned if everyone seems different from you!) We are each on unique journeys. But as your group travels together, you will help each other grow.

Make sure the environment for your Bible study group is welcoming.

- Set up room(s) so participants can easily transition from large to small groups.
- Set appropriate lighting so the videos may easily be viewed while members take notes.

- Make sure that everyone feels welcome. If your study group is large, you may want to appoint greeters to help welcome and direct people.
- Serve lemonade and light refreshments as people arrive for the first session.
- Nothing like total silence makes a room feel awkward! Soft music playing in the background is a great idea to set the tone for your study, so select it carefully. Make sure the volume is set so that participants can easily talk to each other as they arrive.

Registration

- Plan for on-site registration. Meet with your pastor or other appropriate staff member to discuss how to provide member books for each of the participants. In some cases the church may pay for the books, or you may need to collect money during your first meeting.
- Provide name tags for participants. If you choose to give different name tags to visitors, make them subtly different so no one will stick out like a sore thumb!

Weekly Schedule

Each group session is designed to take approximately one hour and includes both small-group discussion and large-group video teaching. Each weekly session includes several components:

- *Welcome* (5 min.): Show opening video clips, featuring Tianne Moon, to the entire study group at the start of each week's session. Using the opening clip is optional, but it introduces the weekly time together and leads into small-group discussion. In some larger settings, these clips are more appropriately shared with small-group leaders.
- *Small-Group Discussion* (20 min.): Each session includes a small-group activity which generates discussion (the majority of the small-group time). Encourage participants to share how they are applying the previous week's home assignments. Small-group discussions should always close with prayer.
- *Large-Group Video Teaching* (25-30 min.): Tianne introduces new material for study in next week's home assignments. Participants can follow along and take notes on the member book viewer guides.
- *Closing*: End each session by sharing the closing video. Remind participants of any upcoming ministry events or opportunities. Encourage members to complete home assignments. Close with prayer.

Bible Study Leader Responsibilities

The primary task of the Bible study leader is to oversee all registration tasks and to support the small-group leaders.

Prior to week 1:
(See Registration tips on page 113.)
- Plan for on-site registration.
- Display the two promotional posters included in the Leader Kit in high-traffic areas.
- Enlist small-group leaders. Show them the "Leader Training Segment" of the DVD video to introduce the study (7:46 min.).
- Provide name tags for leaders and group members.

Before the Session:
(See Environment tips on page 113.)
- Make sure seating and video equipment are in place.
- Meet briefly with small-group leaders and pray for the leaders, participants, and the study before everyone arrives.

During the Session
- Run all three video clips: opening, large-group video session, and closing. For some churches, the opening and closing segments will be optional. Please choose the option that best fits your group's needs. Viewer guide answers are included in "Tianne's Answers."
- Join one of the groups, sharing in the activities and discussion. Your opinion counts. Let the participants see that you are actively studying with them.
- Be on call to assist small-group leaders should the need arise.

This will be an incredible journey! Begin praying for the participants God will bring to the study. Ask for His wisdom as you prepare to help facilitate. Remember, the goal for participants is not only to complete the Bible study but also to experience the life-changing power of God.

Small-Group Leader Responsibilities

The primary task of each small-group leader is to lead discussion and activities during small-group discussion time.

The small-group leaders' commitment to this study and to the participants is the link that encourages members to stay involved in the six-week course. As a small-group leader, you have the privilege of "breathing life" into this study, enabling participants to grow in their relationships with others and with God. As you consider this task and begin preparing, remember the term …

CPR

Coach

As a small-group leader, you are responsible for encouraging everyone to participate in the small-group discussion. Do this by giving positive feedback when people share and making sure no one dominates the discussion (including you!) Don't be afraid of silences; they give others time to reflect on what God is teaching them.

Secondly, you will need to pace the discussion and allow enough time for prayer requests. Remember that the small-group time should take 20–25 minutes. If you have difficulty both facilitating and serving as timekeeper, ask someone in your group to watch the time.

Pray

Encourage participants to keep prayer requests discreet and concise to allow time for everyone to share. A few ways to do that creatively are to:

- have participants describe each request in five sentences or less.
- ask participants for requests that directly involve group members.
- ask for requests that pertain to the small group's discussion.

Reach Out

The participants in your group will depend on you to reach out to them through preparation and contact.

Prepare all activity materials in advance. Read through each week's activity and discussion questions prior to meeting. Be ready to greet and initiate conversation with your group members as they arrive.

Contact your small-group members at least once during each week of study—especially anyone who was absent or who shared a specific prayer request.

Don't worry if the thought of "breathing life" into this study is overwhelming for you or makes you feel inadequate. Remember that the ultimate Breath of Life is Jesus Christ who lives in you, and He is eager and willing to work through you to help others grow and enjoy their relationship with Him!

Directions are for the small-group leader unless otherwise noted.

Before the Session

1. Copy and cut apart enough Cue Card activities so that each member will receive one card (p. 122). (Some members will receive the same question.)

The Cue Cards will contain one of the following questions or statements:

- Why did you decide to participate in this study?
- What do you hope to gain from this study?
- What is the last thing you fixed or tried to fix in your home? Were you successful?
- Name three things that make you smile.
- Describe your ideal sunglasses.
- Which tool do you use most often in your home?

2. (Bible study leader) As participants arrive, make sure each receives a member book and a name tag.

During the Session

1. (Bible study leader) Welcome everyone before verbally dividing participants into small groups. (Hint: Write numbers on participants' name tags which correspond with each discussion group: Group 1, Group 2, and so forth).

2. (Bible study leader) Show session 1 overview (5:30 min.) to the large group.

3. (Bible study leader) Dismiss participants to their small groups.

4. Pass around a copy of the small-group roster (p. 127) so that each person can fill out the contact information. Small-group leaders should keep the roster to use to contact group members during the week.

5. The first week's goal is to allow small-group members to get to know one another. Unfortunately, many are timid about introducing themselves to a group. The Cue Cards activity will help alleviate that fear by guiding members through introductions. While the roster is passed, distribute a Cue Card to each member.

6. Ask each person to introduce herself and answer the Cue Card question or respond to the Cue Card direction.

7. Call on the group to share prayer requests. Since time is limited, ask members to share briefly. (See p. 115, "Small-Group Leader Responsibilities," for tips.)

8. Close in prayer.

9. Ask participants to return to the large group for video instruction. For the sake of time, encourage them to move quickly.

10. (Bible study leader) Show session 1 video (23:58 min.) and the closing video (7:01 min.) for session 1.

11. (Bible study leader) Dismiss with prayer.

SESSION TWO

During the Session

1. (Bible study leader) Show session 2 overview (3:02 min.) to the large group or to your small-group leaders.
2. (Bible study leader) Dismiss participants to their small groups.
3. Add newcomers to your small-group roster and welcome them.
4. Ask members to turn to the Lightning Words activity on page 123.

Say, "Application takes place when we reflect on our learning. This activity is designed to allow us to reflect on this week's study."

5. Have each member circle the first letter of her first, middle, and last names. For example, Sharon Alice Rice would circle an S, A, and R. (See the example at the right.)
6. Instruct members to write a word or phrase from their study that "struck" them this week. That word or phrase should begin with the corresponding letter in their name. For instance, Sharon might write "seeing life through God's eyes" in the S block because the phrase reminds her that her perspective has been skewed.
7. If time allows, give participants the opportunity to share their lightning words and concepts.
8. Review the assignments from week 1 through discussion:

Say, "On day 1, we looked at the importance of being part of a group of people who have similar interests. What are some of your interests, passions, and hobbies? What groups are you a part of because of these interests?"

Say, "On day 2, we looked at how Paul viewed the difficult circumstances in his life. What are some difficult circumstances—no matter how trivial or overwhelming they seem—that God is currently using in your life? What are you learning through these circumstances?"

Say, "On day 3, we discussed competition. What are some areas in which you feel competitive? Describe a time when this competitiveness became a negative factor."

9. Close with prayer before returning to the large group.
10. (Bible study leader) Show session 2 video (24:08 min.) and the closing video (5:26 min.).
11. (Bible study leader) Dismiss with prayer.

SESSION THREE

During the Session

1. (Bible study leader) Show session 3 overview (3:28 min.) to the large group.

2. (Bible study leader) Dismiss participants to their small groups.

3. Ask members to turn to page 124. Fill in the first pyramid together.

4. Say, "Tianne challenges us to search for the bottom line in our assignments. Bottom-Line Pyramids will help us to identify and apply those primary principles and lessons."

5. Guide members to work on a pyramid:

- Say, "On the top line of the pyramid, we will write a word or concept from this week's study." For example, write "humility" on the top line of a pyramid.

- Say, "On the second line, write a verse that defines, supports, or relates to humility. We can write Philippians 2:3 from our homework or choose verses such as Ephesians 4:2 or 1 Peter 5:5-6." Ask members to write Philippians 2:3 on the second tier.

- Say, "On the third line, let's write a principle or lesson we can learn from the concept and verse. From Philippians 2:3, we could write, "Don't assume that I am better than anyone else." Ask participants to write the statement on the third tier.

- Say, "On the fourth line, we will look back at our concept, verse, and general principle to determine the "bottom line" for each of us. This will be very specific and practical—"what this means for me." Explain what the concept of humility as presented in Philippians 2:3 means to you. Ask members to fill in the bottom tier with their explanations.

6. If time allows, allow participants to complete and share a second pyramid.

Encourage participants to complete the third pyramid on their own time.

7. Review week 2:

- Ask, "Which of the Bible study tools have you found most helpful?"

- Say, "On day 1, we looked at the importance of living in unity. How do you normally respond to people whose opinions differ from yours?"

- Say, "On day 2, we discussed that in our relationship with God, obedience is the ultimate evidence of humility. Describe a time when you found it difficult to obey God."

- Say, "In Philippians 2:12, Paul instructed us to 'work out your salvation.' How would you explain this in your own words?"

- Say "On day 4, Paul likened us to 'stars in the universe.' What are some examples of how followers of Christ are shining like stars? How has our light dimmed?"

- Say, "On day 5, we examined the qualities of good friendships. Which of these qualities do you need to develop?"

8. Close with prayer; return to large group.

9. (Bible study leader) Show session 3 video (26:33 min.) and the closing video (5:58 min.).

10. (Bible study leader) Dismiss with prayer.

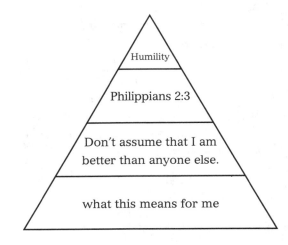

SESSION FOUR

Before the Session
Gather enough crayons or colored pencils for everyone in your group.

During the Session
1. (Bible study leader) Show session 4 overview (2:46 min.) to the large group.
2. (Bible study leader) Dismiss participants to small groups.
3. Say, "During group session this week, we will focus on the eight Bible study tools."
4. Ask members to turn to the Toolbox activity on page 125, and quickly review the names of the eight Bible study tools.
5. Ask members to think about the most common tools they use around the house. It is important that they list tools they use personally and not tools they just see others using so that the connections made will be personal and relevant. (Hammers, nails, and screwdrivers count, but mixers, hair dryers, and cell phones do too.)

Ask the women to match an everyday tool with one of the eight Bible study tools in terms of similar use or appearance. The goal is to create a mental image of the Bible study tool so that when they have trouble remembering what each tool does, they can use the visual as a clue. For instance:

The **Application Tool** is like a glue gun because it allows us to apply truth to our own lives just as a glue gun helps us apply dried flowers to a craft project.

The **Prayer Tool** is like a ladder because it allows us to reach for help and support just as a ladder helps us reach higher levels.

The **Organization Tool** is like a grocery list because it organizes ideas into a list or a diagram.

The **Question Tool** is like a key because it helps us unlock the details of a passage.

Give members 10 minutes to complete the comparisons and draw visuals. Encourage women to share their comparisons and visuals with the group. Be sure to discuss at least one visual that would be appropriate for each of the eight Bible study tools.

6. Review what you have learned this week:
- Ask, "What are some circumstances that replaced your joy with anger, worry, fear, jealousy, or stress this week?"
- Ask, "How did you adjust your perspective so you could still experience joy in the midst of those other emotions?"
- Say, "The pressure of having to prove ourselves can rob us of joy. What are some areas in which you feel you have to prove yourself?"
- Ask, "What do you plan to apply to your life as a result of your study?"

7. Close with prayer and return to the large group.
8. (Bible study leader) Show session 4 video (22:46 min.) and the closing video (5:09 min.).
9. (Bible study leader) Dismiss with prayer.

SESSION FIVE

Before the Session
Gather enough crayons or colored pencils for everyone in your group.

During the Session
1. (Bible study leader) Show the session 5 overview (1:52 min.) to the large group.
2. (Bible study leader) Dismiss participants to their small groups.
3. Ask members to turn to the My Race activity on page 126. Say, "During this session you will have an opportunity to illustrate the important concepts you have been studying in Philippians 3."
4. Instruct each member to use what she has learned in week 4 to add details to this illustration so that it resembles her race to attain the prize to which Paul refers in Philippians 3:12-21. Remind them to add details that reflect the lessons and principles we have been sharing.
5. Encourage participants to be creative and specific with their illustrations.
   Examples may include:
   - A backpack beside the race track (forget what is behind and press ahead).
   - A runner with a backpack on her shoulders (carrying weight of past mistakes).
   - A cross at the finish line (the prize of an intimate relationship with Christ).
   - A person with last year's trophy (the temptation to bask in past success).
6. If time allows, let participants share their illustrations.
7. Encourage participants to save this visual to represent the truths they have learned through this study and as a reminder to apply those truths to their lives.
8. Review week 4:
   - As a group, list the eight Bible study tools. Ask, "Which tool do you find the most challenging?"
   - Say, "On day 2, we talked about pressing toward the goal. How can focusing on past accomplishments be a distraction?"
   - Ask, "What are some past failures that cause you to lose sight of your goal? Why are they so distracting?"
   - Ask, "How do you deal with conflict? How do you want to improve the way you react to conflict?"
9. Close with prayer and dismiss members to large group.
10. (Bible study leader) Show the session 5 teaching video (21:51 min.) and the closing video (2:01 min.).
11. (Bible study leader) Dismiss with prayer.

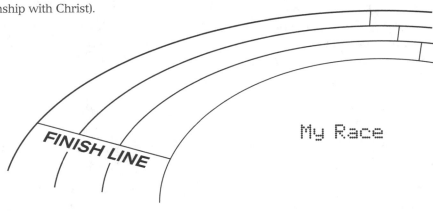

FINISH LINE

My Race

SESSION SIX

During the Session

1. (Bible study leader) Show session 6 overview (2:06 min.) to the large group.

2. (Bible study leader) Dismiss participants to their small groups.

3. Allow participants an opportunity to summarize the lessons and principles God has revealed to them during this study. The Bad News/Good News activity will help to review the major principles of Philippians.

Ask members to turn to the Bad News/Good News activity on page 126. Instruct participants to summarize what they have learned. For example:

- Week 1: Bad News—we can rarely change our circumstances. Good News—our purpose impacts our perspective on those circumstances.

- Week 2: Bad News—we may not always agree with our families or fellow Christians. Good News—when we practice humility in all relationships, we learn to live in unity with them anyway.

- Week 3: Bad News—my heritage, appearance, achievements, possessions, and spirituality may not be impressive. Good News—none of those things measures my worth as a child of God.

- Week 4: Bad News—I have many obstacles in my past that can make me feel guilty and unworthy of serving Christ. Good News—because Christ died for me, I can forget the past and know that He has forgiven me eternally.

- Week 5: Bad News—I am emotional and can allow emotions to control me. Good News—I can replace the tendency to dwell on my emotions with God's promises to love, forgive, and transform me.

4. Ask volunteers to share their responses.

5. Review week 5.

- Say, "On day 1 Paul talked about dealing with worry. What makes you worry?"

- Say, "On day 2, Paul talked about the importance of our thoughts. What do you think about when your mind wanders?"

- Ask, "When have you felt content or discontent? How did your feelings affect your outlook on life?"

- Say, "On day 3, Paul reminded us of the importance of sharing each other's troubles. Who has God brought into your life to help you through difficulties?"

- Ask, "What has God taught you through this study?"

- Ask, "What is a circumstance that threatens to rob you of joy? What have you learned from this study that will help you experience joy in the midst of all circumstances?"

6. Encourage group members to stay in contact with each other as they continue to be involved in other women's ministry activities and church ministries.

7. Close with prayer and return to the large group.

8. (Bible study leader) Show the session 6 teaching video (19:46 min.) and closing video (5:48 min.). Make appropriate closing comments.

9. (Bible study leader) Dismiss with prayer.

Why did you decide to participate in this study?

What do you hope to gain from this study?

What is the last thing you fixed or tried to fix in your home?

Were you successful?

Name three things that make you smile.

Describe your ideal sunglasses.

Which tool do you use most often in your home?

A-B   C-D   E-F

G-H   I-J   K-L

M-N   O-P   Q-R

S-T   U-V   WXYZ

Bottom-Line Pyramid

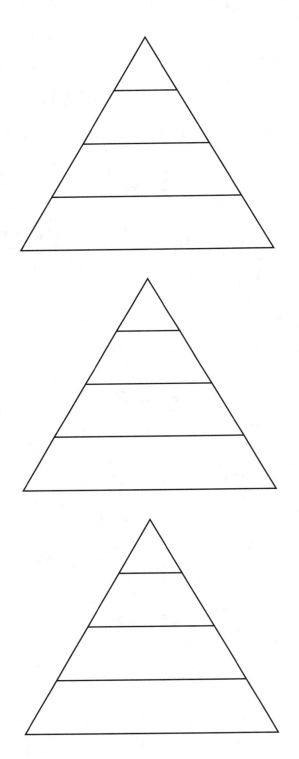

My Bible Study Toolbox

Bible Study Tool	Everyday tool	Comparison	Picture/Visual
The *Question Tool* is like a(n)		because	
The *Application Tool* is like a(n)		because	
The *Creative Tool* is like a(n)		because	
The *Scripture Tool* is like a(n)		because	
The *Relationship Tool* is like a(n)		because	
The *Organization Tool* is like a(n)		because	
The *Prayer Tool* is like a(n)		because	
The *Resource Tool* is like a(n)		because	

My Race

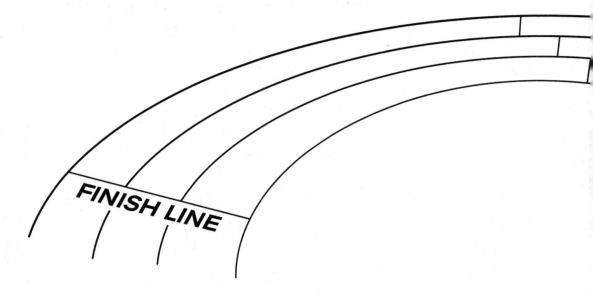

FINISH LINE

(Session 5, My Race)

Bad News, Good News

	The Bad News is …	The Good News is …
Week 1		
Week 2		
Week 3		
Week 4		
Week 5		

Small-Group Roster

Name	Address/E-Mail	Phone	Session					
			1	2	3	4	5	6

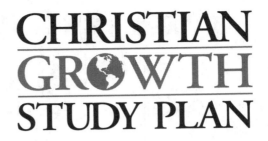

CHRISTIAN GROWTH STUDY PLAN

In the **Christian Growth Study Plan (formerly Church Study Course),** this book *Enjoy: A Thirst-Quenching Look at Philippians* is a resource for course credit in the subject area Biblical Studies the Christian Growth category of plans. To receive credit, read the book, complete the learning activities, show your work to your pastor, a staff member or church leader, then complete the following information. This page may be duplicated. Send the completed page to:

Christian Growth Study Plan
• **One LifeWay Plaza; Nashville, TN 37234-0117**
• **FAX: (615)251-5067**
• **Email:** *cgspnet@lifeway.com*
For information about the Christian Growth Study Plan, refer to the Christian Growth Study Plan Catalog. It is located online at *www.lifeway.com/cgsp*. If you do not have access to the Internet, contact the Christian Growth Study Plan office (1.800.968.5519) for the specific plan you need for your ministry.

Enjoy: A Thirst-Quenching Look at Philippians

COURSE NUMBER: CG-1050

PARTICIPANT INFORMATION

Social Security Number (USA ONLY-optional)	Personal CGSP Number*	Date of Birth (MONTH, DAY, YEAR)
– –	– –	– –

Name (First, Middle, Last)		Home Phone
		– –

Address (Street, Route, or P.O. Box)	City, State, or Province	Zip/Postal Code

Please check appropriate box: ❏ Resource purchased by self ❏ Resource purchased by church ❏ Other

CHURCH INFORMATION

Church Name		
Address (Street, Route, or P.O. Box)	City, State, or Province	Zip/Postal Code

CHANGE REQUEST ONLY

❏ Former Name		
❏ Former Address	City, State, or Province	Zip/Postal Code
❏ Former Church	City, State, or Province	Zip/Postal Code

Signature of Pastor, Conference Leader, or Other Church Leader	Date

*New participants are requested but not required to give SS# and date of birth. Existing participants, please give CGSP# when using SS# for the first time. Thereafter, only one ID# is required. Mail to: Christian Growth Study Plan, One LifeWay Plaza, Nashville, TN 37234-0117. Fax: (615)251-5067.

Rev. 3-03